The Great American Gun Argument

by

Michael R. Weisser

in collaboration with

William A. Weisser

Volume 4: Guns in America

Published by:

TeeTee Press
Ware MA 01082

Cover design by Damonza

ISBN: 0692336354
ISBN-13: 978-0692336359

10 9 8 7 6 5 4 3 2 1

First Edition

To my parents, Jean and Saul Weisser,
who taught me how to read and write.

CONTENTS

CHAPTER 1

TAKES TWO SIDES TO MAKE AN ARGUMENT

My father's favorite gadget when I was growing up was a Kodak Super 8mm home movie camera. He bought his first camera at some point after I was born and then added a Revere Super 8 projector to the arsenal. He sent the film away to be developed, and it was always a big deal when one of the yellow packages containing a developed reel would be delivered by the mailman (who in those days, the 1950's, made both morning and afternoon home deliveries), because it meant that after dinner we would be treated to the latest film of the family's doings; a party, a backyard barbeque, a trip somewhere with everyone waving from inside the Packard and later the Dodge, and so forth. We didn't own a television until 1954 or '55 so a home movie screen made out of a bed sheet that we taped onto the wall was a big deal.

The earliest home movie of me was taken in June or July of 1950 when I was not quite six years old. I was standing in front of my grandfather's fruit store with a big smile on my face. Why was I so happy? Because I was wearing my black cowboy hat with a white braid around the rim, and I was twirling my silver-plated revolver around in my hand. The revolver was actually plastic and it wasn't quite the size of a real gun. But that gun and its leather holster was always on me or near me from that day until it was replaced a few years later by my first baseball glove, a Rawlings G600 Marty Marion model, the shortstop of the St. Louis Cardinals even though in Little League I played outfield.

I still have the Rawlings glove even though I haven't played baseball in about fifty years. I have no idea what happened to the plastic revolver which probably was made to look like the gun carried by Roy Rogers or Tom Mix. But it doesn't matter what I did with the toy guns because I bought my first real gun when I was twelve years old and I've been buying and playing around with real guns ever since. How many guns have I personally owned since I picked up that first Smith & Wesson K-frame at a flea market in Florida in 1956? Without exaggeration I would say somewhere between four and five hundred. And I'm not counting the fifteen thousand or so guns that moved through my retail stores over the years; I'm only counting the guns that were personally owned by me.

I just bought a Model 17 Smith. It's a beautiful gun with a six-inch barrel, polished with a deep, royal-blue finish and shoots 22LR with an accuracy unmatched by any other untuned factory gun right out of the box. The piece is about thirty years old and the moment I got it to my shop I went downstairs and put six rounds through the gun in the little test range that I built a few years back. I grouped five of the six shots at one-half inch at six yards. Will I ever shoot the gun again? Maybe yes, maybe no, it doesn't really matter and I don't care. It's a beautiful gun. Saw it, wanted it, bought it. Get it?

Have I spent $150,000 on guns over the last fifty-eight years? That's a low estimate. But when you stop and think about it, while the total may sound impressive to people who don't own guns, it works out to a bit over $2,500 a year, which is a little over $200 a month. Shit, two hundred bucks is monthly beer money, or cigarettes, or both. And I never was much of a drinker and I stopped smoking when I was fifty years old. So the fact that I averaged a couple of hundred bucks a month on a habit that began when I was a few months shy of six years old and has continued ever since isn't such a big deal. I know guys who in the same time-period or less in which I bought and sold four or five hundred guns, bought and sold two or three thousand, or maybe only sold a thousand of them and the remaining couple of thousand are still stacked around the house. I used to know a guy who lived in South Jersey, out in the Pine Barrens, who had the good sense to insure all his guns. When his house burned to the ground and all the guns were destroyed, the insurance company paid him a lot more for the guns than what they gave him for the two-bedroom dump which he called home.

Guns aren't my only hobby. I used to be a pretty good golfer and I still indulge myself by ponying up some cash each year for the dues that lets me play at a really beautiful course when, truth to tell, I'd probably be just as happy hacking at the local muni through the front nine. I also occasionally take my Nikon with its four lenses into the woods to shoot various flora and fauna, even though digital technology robs me of the opportunity I used to have to develop my own pictures. But golf and nature photography are "adult" activities; I had no interest in either when I was a kid. Guns, on the other hand, were with me before I even started school. And they are still with me now that I am long out of school.

But let's go back to the beginning.

The first real movie I ever remember seeing was a Western called *Shane*, starring Alan Ladd. It hit the theaters in 1953. I might have seen *Treasure Island* and a few other early Disney movies or cartoons around the same time, but the climactic gunfight between the good guy, Alan Ladd, and the bad guy, Jack Palance, stayed with me for years. I don't think a week went by during my childhood when I didn't strap on my silver gun and black leather holster and pretend to be filling Jack Palance up with lead. I should add, by the way, that I was born and raised in Washington, D.C., the Nation's Capital, and the furthest out west I ever travelled in those years was to eat Sunday lunch at Barbara Fritchie's Restaurant which still serves patrons in Frederick, MD, about 45 miles from my house. In other words, I might have gotten my first taste of guns from watching Western movies, but I certainly had really no idea about where these cowboy adventures actually took place.

On the other hand, by the time I was eleven years old, in 1955, I was a member of an NRA-sponsored rifle club which practiced each Friday in a rifle range in the basement of McFarland Junior High. My brother was a student at McFarland, and every Friday afternoon I would trot over from my grammar school on Farragut Avenue and join him in the basement of McFarland where we shot bolt-action 22-caliber rifles that had been used by the Army as training weapons during both world wars.

When team practice finished, my brother and I and other members of the team were allowed to pack up the rifles and take them home for the weekend to be cleaned. This was a good deal for the coach, because he didn't have to clean the rifles, and it was an even better deal for us kids because we got to play all weekend with real guns. My brother Billy and I walked about a mile home from McFarland carrying the rifle in a cloth case and it was impossible for anyone to mistake the contents of that case for anything other than what was in the case, namely, a gun. We didn't walk home with this rifle in Topeka, or Rapid City, or Cheyenne. *We walked up Georgia Avenue in the middle of Washington, D.C.* If you wanted to play around with a gun in the 1950's, that's what you did. You carried it home from school no matter where you lived.

I start off with this story because I want everyone to understand what guns meant to me and to everyone else who used them or owned them in the years following World War II. My father served in the war, he participated in the first amphibious landing in the Pacific's Marshall chain on a crummy little island called Kwajelein. This island was chosen as the first amphibious landing in the Pacific because it was lightly defended and the Navy wanted to try out some amphibious landing techniques under combat conditions so that they wouldn't fuck up the landings the way they had fucked up again and again when they tried to put troops ashore in North Africa the previous year. I don't believe my father waded through the surf while bullets were still zipping around; he remained shipboard until the island was completely under U.S. control. But he knew other guys who hit the beach at Kwajelein and also he knew some of the guys who didn't come back to the ship.

My father, Saul Weisser, returned from the Pacific theater a few months before I was born and the men he served with in the Marines and the Navy remained his lifelong friends. And while the ones who lived in and around D.C. got together all the time for birthdays, holidays and other social events, I never recall them talking about the war. They argued about politics, they lamented the fact that Washington ("first in war, first in peace and last in the American League") was home to the absolutely worst Major League Baseball team until the advent decades later of the New York Mets, and they always tried to outdo each other when it came to who could grill and serve the best backyard steaks. But they never talked about the war.

Also, none of them owned guns. Now, all their kids had arsenals of toy weapons and it was a *rite de passage* to get your hands on a Daisy Red Ryder BB gun at some point while you were growing up. I recall that the hardware store two blocks from our house sold them for nine or ten bucks. But the adult men around me never owned guns and they never talked about guns even though my father's best friend took us to see every Western shoot-'em-up movie, including *Shane*, that played at the local RKO Keith's. And the reason they never talked about guns and never owned guns was because they associated guns not with protecting their families against crime, not as a statement about their 2nd Amendment rights, and certainly not as a tool to be used to shoot a squirrel out of a tree. These guys didn't talk about guns because they associated guns with the death and injury that they but not others escaped during World War II. Which is why they didn't have good memories about the war. Which is why they didn't feel good about guns.

Many years later when my father was retired and he and my mother had long since moved away from D.C., I happened to visit them and walked into their house in New Jersey carrying a Ruger Mini-14. I had just bought the peppy little rifle at a gun show in Pennsylvania, it was a new and unique rifle design at the time, and I wanted to show it to my younger brother who was also visiting my parents the same day. As I carried it past my father who was lying on the couch catching a quick snooze before lunch, he woke up, saw the gun and said, "Hey, that's the gun I trained with during the war."

Actually, he had trained with the M-1 carbine, the mini-version of the Garand, which was similar in look and feel to the Mini-14 that Bill Ruger designed at some point following the War. I didn't want to explain the difference to my father who was just about to doze back off to sleep, but for a moment his eyes caught mine and he gave me a little wink. And what that wink represented was two things: a momentary but deeply-vital emotional connection between father and son, and my father's understanding that because I had been spared the horrors that he associated with guns in the war, I could still walk around with a gun and have a good time. If you were the son of a World War II veteran, and just about every male of age served in that war so being a veteran's son wasn't such an unusual state of affairs, you knew that your father had probably spent time learning how to shoot guns. But you also knew that guns represented something much different for him than for you.

Most American men who survived service in the war went back home to the farms and small towns where they lived. And this was because a majority of Americans lived on farms and in small towns in the years leading up to the war. So most of those guys, unlike my father, needed to keep a gun around their home. But within one decade after the end of World War II, all of this began to change. Thanks to the G.I. Bill, the suburbs, which contained less than 15% of America's total population in the 1930's, grew to 25% by 1950 and by 1960 counted more than one-third of the entire US population. By 1970, more Americans lived in suburbs than anywhere else. Not surprisingly, it was during these two decades, 1950–1970, that the movie industry pumped out thousands of cowboy movies that largely fueled a nostalgia for the West because the West and its cowboys had disappeared. In 1968 I spent an afternoon with the elderly grandmother of one of my childhood friends listening to the woman recount her memories of the trip across the country in a Conestoga wagon hauled by four mules. Her trip took two months. I met the old gal at her grand-daughter's home in Boulder, CO, having just driven from Chicago to the West Coast and back to Colorado in less than a week.

Now we move ahead two decades and I am walking out of a theater where I had just seen a flick while on vacation in Paris, France. It was called *Don't Touch the White Woman* and it starred two of my personal screen favorites, Marcello Mastroianni and Catherine Deneuve. You would imagine that this film would have been a typical Mastroianni-Deneuve vehicle about unrequited love, Paris or Rome cafes, the bourgeois this or the bourgeois that. Actually it was about Custer's Last Stand, complete with the Indians winning and the cavalry guys getting sliced up. But the movie wasn't set at the Little Big Horn or any other location in the United States. It took place in an enormous hole in the ground in the middle of Paris (which actually did bear something of a resemblance to the Montana landscape), which was where the old vegetable market known as *Les Halles* was being replaced by a hideous vertical shopping and cultural mall named after the late French Prime Minister Georges Pompidou. The construction of the Pompidou Center, as it was known, marked the transformation of Paris from a beautiful, medieval city with narrow, winding, cobblestoned streets to just another overly-expensive urban sprawl designed to accommodate the car. And the Indians in the movie represented the residents of the old neighborhood who were fighting against the government's attempt (by sending in the cavalry) to push them out.

So the movie, which really wasn't all that good, was an allegory on the theme of social displacement and urban change, but I went to see it because one of my French friends had told me that I would enjoy seeing how the French dealt with Custer's Last Stand.

And what I pointed out to him was that it took the French to make a movie about Custer that, for the first time, transformed what had been one of America's authentic heroes who died protecting us from savage hordes into a villain who led our troops on a campaign to slaughter and destroy the real Americans, the native Americans, who were only doing what they had to do to protect their land.

We glorified the West in the 1950's because this was a decade in which we glorified everything having to do with the growth of America. But it was also the decade in which we consolidated the economic gains of the war years and, by dint of the G.I. Bill, the federal highway trust fund, the oil-depletion allowance and a few other government baubles that looted the Treasury while being given out to the deserving few and a few of the deserving many, created the world's first, truly middle-class society whose economic growth was increasingly tied to the purchase of consumer goods (when we say "consumer goods" it's shorthand to describe things we really don't need).

And one of these consumer products for which there's no real need is guns. There are other Western countries that allow their citizens to own small arms, but the sale and ownership of guns in places like Italy and Austria, which are two of the more liberal

European countries in terms of guns, is nothing like the USA. You'll find a gun shop in Italy if you know where to look and if the owner will unlock the door and let you inside. The gun store I visited in Austria had no display windows on the outside of the store and almost no guns displayed on the inside, for that matter. Want to buy a gun in the United States? Walk into just about any hardware store or pawn shop or discount, never mind the gun shops themselves. I have found nice gun shops in the back of laundromats, delis and gasoline stations. There's a gun shop in New Hampshire that shares space with a store selling retail funeral caskets.

You don't even need to leave your house to buy all the guns you want. All you need to do is fill out a simple government application known as a C&R, which stands for Curios and Relics, enclose a check for thirty bucks, and assuming that you aren't a felon or fall into one of those other "prohibited" categories for gun ownership, you can sit at home, peruse the internet and purchase any legal firearm as long as it was first manufactured more than 50 years ago. How many guns are floating around that were manufactured prior to May 22, 1964, which is the date that I am writing the first draft of this book? Probably fifty million or more. And most of them still work. I'm looking right now to buy a Walther PP or PPK in

.380 caliber, and I'll probably spend some time after I finish a few more pages to see if I can go online and track one down.

And if I don't want to bother to get a C&R License from the Feds, or if you happen to be one of those "prohibited" persons who isn't allowed by law to buy or own guns, you can go online to websites like armslist.com and find hundreds of guns within a two hour's drive of your home that belong to sellers who more than likely will sell you the piece if and when you show up with the case. Right now I'm engaged in an email exchange with a guy who lives about thirty miles from me and wants to unload (as in to sell, not to take out ammunition from) a very good-looking Colt Trooper revolver for a pretty fair price. If he wants to go through the trouble of filling out the online form required for private sales in my state, that's fine. If he just wants to give me the gun without the paperwork nonsense, that's fine too. One of the gun control advocacy organizations published a report in which they estimated that in Washington State alone, more than 4,000 prohibited persons were able to get guns through bypassing the federal NICS check system, and while I'm not sure if their numbers are all that exact, the bottom line is that just about anyone who wants to get a gun in American can do so without creating any kind of a stir.[1]

Oh, and by the way, before we end this section on how to buy a gun in America, let me give you another option if you don't want to use the internet because of all this talk about NSA spying and so forth and so on. I estimate there are 3,000–4,000 public gun clubs in the United States; the term "gun club" being a euphemism for a place with a bar and a berm. Some of these clubs are really nice gun ranges with skeet, trap, long-distance rifle and tactical or handgun shooting areas, they are all connected in some way or another to the NRA, and most of them can be found in the range section of the website of the NSSF. But most of these local clubs are kind of like the local VFW: a place for the guys to hang out, pop a few tops, shoot the shit a bit and, from time to time, actually shoot their guns. The only times these clubs get busy is a few days before the hunting season when everyone shows up to "sight their gun in," whether they actually get out to the woods or not. Show up on a busy range day with some cash in your pocket and see how difficult it is to buy a gun.

When I first got interested in the gun argument, I discovered that most of the organizations who promote gun control are located in places where it's next to impossible to purchase a gun. I'm talking about Washington, D.C. and New York City, which together contain the media, the personalities and what are called the "influencers" who shape the national debate, at least from the gun control point of view. The researchers upon whom this community relies for their information about guns are somewhat more dispersed geographically, but most of the public health and other scholars, if not nearly all of them, live and work in environments where guns are, for the most part, simply unknown. So people from these kinds of backgrounds simply can't imagine a situation in which guns are can be purchased as easily and normally as one would go about buying tires for your car. If it's really that easy to get a gun, no wonder so many of them fall into the wrong hands.

On the other hand, because guns are so readily available outside of a few metropolitan areas that to talk about the lack of gun "control" in the United States as compared to other countries, is to do nothing more than indulge in a bad joke. But let's briefly indulge ourselves. In nearly every other industrialized country, long guns—rifles, shotguns— are permitted but usually restricted to one or two weapons per family, and in many countries are not allowed to be kept at home. As for handguns, they are almost entirely *verboten* from personal ownership, or are limited to target guns in only the smallest calibers, such as 22. And even in countries that have somewhat liberal laws and regulations on handgun ownership, like Italy or Austria, the cops basically know the location of every single weapon that was sold legally, and private transfers of handguns between individuals is simply unknown.

In the United States the ability of the police to know who owns the guns is the exception, not the rule. And it's so much the exception that, roughly speaking, at least two-thirds of the entire American population lives in states where there is no ability to track gun ownership at all. While all counter-top gun purchases that take place in a federally-licensed dealer's location require a background check with the FBI before the gun can be transferred to the customer, the background check covers the purchaser, not the gun. The only information about the weapon is whether it is a handgun or a long gun (any firearm with a barrel length of less than 16 inches is a handgun), and the FBI does not even aggregate this meager data for reporting purposes. And if you walk into a shop and purchase ten AR-15 rifles so that you can lead a brigade up a latter-day version of San Juan Hill, the FBI only knows that you purchased a long gun, not whether you are getting ready to invade Poland or send a flying squad into the local bank. Meanwhile, only a handful of states require background checks on private gun transfers; the statement above that two-thirds of all gun ownership cannot be checked is probably an over-estimation and should not be necessarily accepted as true.

In defending the very strict licensing procedure for handguns that now covers Washington, D.C., the District's Chief of Police, Cathy Lanier, noted that an online list of all gun owners would make it easier for officers, when responding to a distress call, to know whether they were entering a home where guns might be found. This statement was disputed by the NRA's witness, Gary Kleck, who opined, among other things, that Chief Lanier's long experience as a police officer and administrator conferred upon her absolutely no credibility as an expert witness on gun control.[2] But what is interesting about the Chief's testimony was the fact that what she was recommending is standard procedure in police operations outside the United States. Of course, outside the United States there's nothing known as the 2nd Amendment.

What is all this hue and cry about the 2nd Amendment? Regardless of my point of view, my biases or anything else, if I'm going to write a book about Americans and their guns, I have to say *something* about the 2nd Amendment. This is for the simple reason that there is no other part of the Constitution which is mentioned as frequently in current public debate about anything, let alone guns.

For example, I did a keyword search on Google for May, 2014 (a period which covered an extremely high-profile shooting incident in California) and the phrase "2nd Amendment" was searched nearly 200,000 times in the 31-day period, while the term "Bill of Rights" was searched 114,000 and "1st Amendment" was searched 74,000 times. I suspect that this search traffic profile would hold true for any period in the last few years. Which doesn't mean that most people are interested in the 2nd Amendment per se, rather in most cases they are interested in something having to do with guns. And for the most part they want to pick up some verbiage or another that defends their "right" to own a gun, because as Philip Cook has observed, when it comes to the public debate about guns, "the pro-gun side has the upper hand."[3] The point being, that they want to contribute their two cents to the argument about guns, and one of the issues that comes up time and time again during the gun argument is the 2nd Amendment, whether it's germane to the argument or not (it's usually not).

The other reason that the phrase "2nd Amendment" gets so many internet searches has to do with one thing and one thing only, namely, the propensity of a very small group of Americans to pick up a gun, walk or drive into an area with lots of people, and begin pulling the trigger. The United States is the only Western country in which mass shootings take place on a regular basis; there have been more than 100 persons killed in 7 mass shootings since Columbine in 1999, and while at least 12 other countries have experienced at least one shooting that killed 7 or more people, we are the only country in which episodes of this sort continue to happen again and again and again.[4]

Now, the truth is that these mass shootings don't change the overall numbers on American gun violence to any great or even small degree. For example, the 27 deaths in Sandy Hook on December 14, 2012, added about one-quarter of one percent to the total gun deaths recorded that year. But what does happen is that shootings that garner massive media attention usually provoke some degree of debate about guns, which then turns into the argument about guns, while the daily carnage that adds up to 30,000+ deaths each year usually makes little media impact, hence little public discussion at all, hence no argument about guns. The total number of gun deaths each year—roughly 30,000, two-thirds being suicides—is not much different from the total number of persons killed each year in highway fatalities.[5] When was the last time that anyone attended a mass vigil for someone killed in a car accident?

Not that we don't try to control or diminish highway deaths through a combination of better engineering, seat belts, anti-DUI programs, stronger enforcement and so on. For that matter we have also successfully attacked other public health threats like smoking and, more recently, obesity. But gun violence, although it has been listed as a public health issue since the first list of public health issues was compiled and published in 1980,[6] has never lent itself to any degree of consensus about dealing with the problem, a lack of agreement reflected in those 2nd Amendment internet search numbers cited above. Because it has to be understood that most of the people who search for the 2nd Amendment couldn't really care less about what it says. They are searching for comments about the 2nd Amendment because they want to engage in some fashion or another in the argument about guns and they figure that the 2nd Amendment is a good place to start.

In fact, if you want to understand all the talk about guns and all the arguments about guns from one side and the other, the 2nd Amendment is probably about the worst place to situate yourself because, appearances to the contrary, the gun argument isn't about the 2nd Amendment at all. First of all, everyone believes in the 2nd Amendment, even those who wish it could or should be changed. As much of a Constitutional authority as the former SCOTUS Associate Justice John Paul Stevens may want the text of the Amendment to specify that gun ownership is reserved only for those individuals who serve in a military unit,[7] but note that he doesn't want the Amendment itself thrown out. The truth is that we are a country that simply can't or won't get rid of its guns and therefore the argument over who should have them and how they should be used breaks out every time that someone demonstrates through a fearsome event that he shouldn't have been able either to get his hands on a gun or, once getting his hands on a gun, used it in a terribly unfortunate way.

Notice a gender distinction in the previous paragraph; the use of only the male gender when it comes to speaking about committing violence with guns. This is because only 10% of murder offenders are female, and not all women who kill someone else use a gun.[8] Furthermore, as far back as one can track such events, I can only find rare instances of a multiple shooting, defined by the FBI as an incident in which 4 or more persons were killed, in which the shooter was a woman. Women have become somewhat more violent on an overall basis, with females committing roughly one-quarter of all violent crimes,[9] a proportion that has increased from roughly 14% at the beginning of the new century.[10] But even though the glass ceiling for violent behavior has been pushed upwards, women haven't broken through completely, particularly when we talk about murder, with or without a gun.

I'll return to the gender issue in a few pages, but let's go back to the question of the 2nd Amendment and why it comes up so often in the gun argument. This is the handiwork of the National Rifle Association, which has fashioned its entire side of the gun argument around the self-aggrandizing notion that defending gun ownership is tantamount to defending the Constitution, and who would ever argue with defending that sacred text? Which is far cry from how and why the NRA first got started, even though the 2nd Amendment was already long enshrined in the Bill of Rights.

But before I give a brief history of the NRA, I just want to make sure that everyone understands the title of this book. I use the word "argument" in a very specific way. And what I mean is that there are two sides with two very different positions on the issue of guns, and when these positions come into disagreement, it's the side that makes the most noise, and makes it on a continuous basis, that usually wins. Noise isn't synonymous with evidence, it's not driven by facts, it's just noise. An argument isn't a discussion and it's surely not a debate. The louder and longer you yell, the better the chance that people will listen at least a little bit to what you have to say. I can't think of another public policy issue in which the question of what, if anything, to do about the issue is based on so much noise with so little attention to facts. Which is why guns are the subject of an ongoing argument and not the subject of a debate. But to have an argument you need two sides. So let's pick up our little history of the NRA so that you'll know how and when these two sides came to be.

Ironically, the NRA got started not in opposition to the federal government's control of guns, but as an organization to help defend the government from enemies both domestic and abroad. The organization's founder, a New York lawyer named George Wingate, had served as a General in the Union Army during the Civil War, and was dismayed by the lack of prowess in firearms exhibited by many of the Union troops. Since the Union army was only comprised of troops that were conscripted and trained as state militias (the first peacetime draft resulting in a standing army was in 1940), most regular troops did the bulk of their firearms activity after they reached the battlefield and prepared to fight. The NRA didn't mention anything about the 2nd

Amendment in its founding documents, stating instead that it was committed to promoting and encouraging rifle shooting on a "scientific basis."[11] I should add, parenthetically, that the organization's first shooting range was located at Creedmoor, Long Island, the site of the current state psychiatric hospital which bears the same name.[12]

The NRA didn't swing into the business of defending the 2nd Amendment until the federal government debated and then passed the Gun Control Act of 1968. The only previous gun control measure had been the 1934 National Firearms Act (NFA) that prohibited civilians from owning fully-automatic weapons, as well as certain other types of accessories like silencers and sawed-off shotguns. Actually, it would be a mistake to say that the NFA prohibited ownership of machine guns, because what the law did was to regulate their acquisition and use in ways that made it difficult for such items to be bought and sold in an easy, legal way. The NFA basically established a licensing system for automatic guns which is fairly similar to what exists in most Western countries for all sporting arms, in particular handguns, which is why most other industrialized countries have a tiny fraction of the small arms floating around that we find in the US today.

I own a machine gun, in common parlance usually referred to as a "grease gun," chambered in 9mm with a folding metal stock which allows me to hide it easily under a jacket or carry it in a sling behind my back. I paid roughly a thousand for the gun back in 1994 or 1995, but I also had to pay a $250 registration fee to the Treasury Department and apply for separate state and federal licenses, for which the latter background check and approval took about six months. I can't walk around with the gun concealed but there's no special rules that I need to follow in terms of storing it safely or locking it away.

On the other hand, I can't sell or transfer the gun to anyone except through what is known as a Class III–NFA dealer who also needs additional licenses beyond what is required to conduct business in regular sporting arms. You would think that going through all that rigmarole to purchase and own such a weapon would make the number of automatic weapons floating around to be minimal at best. In fact, the correct number of auto guns owned by people like you and me is anywhere between 60,000 and 1.5 million, but it's probably an impossible number to pin down because the NFA tax stamp that must be purchased for every transaction of an automatic weapon is also required for transfers of all

NFA products; e.g., silencers, handguns with rifle stocks and so forth.[13]

What isn't difficult to pin down are the number of homicides involving an auto-gun that take place each year, or perhaps it would be better to say each decade, or each half-century. It appears that, believe it or not, the last time a fully-automatic weapon was used in a murder was 1947, and I'm not even sure about the reliability of this source.[14] But the bottom line is that the relative scarcity of auto-gun deaths reflects both the relative number of automatic weapons owned by civilians; after all, 250,000 is only one-tenth of one percent of all small arms in the United States. But more to the point, it reflects the rigid licensing infrastructure surrounding automatic weapon ownership, an infrastructure whose design and implementation was in no small measure due to input by the NRA. Indeed, the then-NRA President, Karl Frederick, testified before a Congressional committee in April and May of 1934 during consideration of the bill, and here's what he said:

> I have never believed in the general practice of carrying weapons. I seldom carry one. I have when I felt it was desirable to do so for my own protection. I know that applies in most of the instances where guns are used effectively in self-defense or in places of

business and in the home. I do not believe in the general promiscuous toting of guns. I think it should be sharply restricted and only under licenses.[15]

This rather benign view of the government's role in controlling small arms remained the basic NRA position even when the Feds created an end-to-end licensing system with the Gun Control Act of 1968. For the first time, the government set criteria for gun ownership by establishing definitions of "prohibited persons" who could not own or purchase small arms (e.g., felons, mental defectives) and also restricted firearm sales through the licensing of dealers. The law also mandated that gun purchases or transfers could only occur across state lines through the intervention of a dealer who would receive the gun from the resident of another state and conduct the transfer to a resident of the dealer's state. The NRA not only went along with these provisions, but actively worked with members of Congress in drafting the final bill. If there was any concern that gun owners needed to protect themselves against a loss of their 2nd Amendment rights, it was muted and certainly was not used by the NRA to generate any degree of public opposition against the 1968 law.

The NRA's lack of concern for preserving and strengthening 2nd Amendment rights changed direction in 1977 when a new leadership team, led by Harlon Carter, disavowed the organization's more compromising positions on gun ownership and adopted a more defiant and combative tone as regards government interference with the right to own guns. Carter, who ran the U.S. Border Patrol in the 1950's and then worked for the INS in the 1960's, had been convicted of second-degree murder when, at age seventeen, he confronted a fifteen-year old Hispanic, fatally wounding him with a shotgun blast during a classic stand-your-ground confrontation near Carter's home. Not known for understatement, Carter vigorously and vociferously moved the NRA away from its traditional alliance with hunting and outdoor recreation groups, instead building support around the notion of guns as the citizens' first line of defense against crime.

It wasn't difficult to persuade Americans that crime was a problem in the late 1970's, since the violent crime rate had more than doubled over the previous decade, a function largely of the heroin epidemic spawned by returning veterans from Vietnam. It also didn't help that a "hard line" on crime was sweeping towards Washington in the persona of Ronald Reagan, whose racially-tinged metaphors about the "welfare queen" and other appeals to working-class white resentment against inner-city minorities fed larger fears that things were out of control. An example of how the NRA's new strategy paralleled the swing in the national mood is what happened to Charlton Heston, who by the late 1980's was doing television commercials for the NRA that found him walking down a forbiddingly-dark street in Washington, D.C., intoning about how the nation's capital was "ruled by criminals," while the country's leaders slept comfortably just a few blocks away.

Like most Hollywood actors, Heston started out in the 1950's as a card-carrying liberal, endorsing Democratic candidates, leading the actor's union (Screen Actors Guild) and promoting civil rights and gun control both before and after 1968. He picketed segregated theaters showing his movies and joined a gaggle of Hollywood luminaries for Martin Luther King's March on Washington in 1963. Throughout the 1970's he remained, for the most part, a solid Democrat, both in terms of endorsements and policy positions, and almost agreed to run for U.S. Senate on the Democratic ticket in 1969.

The turning-point for Heston came in 1980 with the election of Reagan and a more conservative approach to both foreign and domestic political affairs. Heston registered as a Republican during Reagan's second term, began speaking out against gun control and doing NRA ads at the same time, and tried as often as he could to get public notice about his views on the "culture war." In the 1990's he became a constant spokesman for the organization and served in the ceremonial position of NRA President from 1998 until 2003. Heston was one of a generation of entertainment figures (Frank Sinatra being another) who moved left to right across the political spectrum in the decades following World War II. But his connection to the NRA was also a function of the organization's drift towards conservative political advocacy which became the centerpiece of NRA marketing strategy in response to the rightward drift of the political spectrum. The rightward shift was particularly evident in the White working-class demographic which, in case you hadn't noticed, was also was the gun-owning demographic.

The full thrust of the NRA's "us" (gun owners) versus "them" (non-gun owners) didn't emerge, however, until the political fight which erupted over the gun control laws that were passed in 1993 and 1994. The first law was known as the Brady bill, so-named for Reagan's press secretary James Brady, who was terribly wounded in an assassination attempt on Reagan in 1981; the second was known as the Assault Weapons Ban, which was part of a large anti-crime initiative promoted by President Clinton and signed into law in 1994. Basically, the Brady bill took away the ability of licensed gun dealers to decide whether customers should be entitled to purchase guns and transferred this authority to the FBI, which established a national call center whose operators, in theory, could check the backgrounds of gun buyers by examining court records in most states. It took five years for the system to become fully operational, and basically what it meant was that transferring a gun to someone who was considered to be a "prohibited person" (felon, mental defective and so forth) could only take place on private, non-licensed terms.

The Assault Weapons Ban probably would not have gained Congressional approval had it not been bundled in a large, anti-crime bill that included an additional 100,000 cops to be spread among many big-city departments and paid for by the federal fisc. The ban on assault weapons meant that gun owners could still own but no longer purchase rifles with certain military-style features, such as flash hiders and bayonet lugs on the barrel, but also limited magazine capacities for all semi-automatic pistols and rifles to 10 rounds. The issue of magazine capacity became a flash-point of the gun debate from then until now.

It's not clear whether the NRA's stance on the Brady bill resulted in the passage of what would be a compromised version from what had originally been introduced. I say that only because the bill had been bubbling around in Congress since it was first introduced in 1987, and keeping alive any kind of legislation for seven years always requires extreme tenacity on the part of the sponsors, regardless of how much noise is made on the other side. But whether they were responsible or not, the NRA has always taken credit for the chief compromise in the law, which saw the elimination of a national waiting-period for handgun sales (first seven, then five, then no days), along with maintaining background checks only for transfers between dealers and buyers, thus leaving the private gun market largely untouched. The NRA did go to court and challenge a provision of the law that required states to conduct background checks if the Federal FBI-NICS system wasn't operational, but by the time that the SCOTUS agreed with the NRA on this point (while finding the rest of the Brady Act constitutional), most states had already or were shortly going to have the FBI doing background checks over the phone.[16]

As I said above, I don't believe that the Assault Weapons Ban would have made it through Congress had it not been bundled in the enormous anti-crime bill (the largest such measure in U.S. history) that Clinton pushed through in 1994. The bill was passed, in fact, just prior to the mid-term elections that saw the Republicans gain control of both houses of Congress for the first time since 1952. The crime bill did not play a central role in the blue-to-red shift in November, 1994 (much more was made out of the Clinton health-care initiative, plus the country was pissed off because of the major-league baseball strike), but again the provisions covering guns in the bill were substantially watered down, and Clinton in his autobiography stated that the NRA's opposition to the law might have cost him a majority in the lower House.[17]

Whether Clinton's view of the NRA's impact on the 1994 election is correct or not, the fact is that 1994 was a watershed year not just for NRA advocacy, but for advocacy efforts on both sides of the gun issue. Because while Sarah Brady and her allies in and out of Congress were unable to get their original version of the bill to the President's desk, the fact that they were able to deliver two gun control within one year, bills that allowed the federal government to actively control a portion of the gun market, as well as control the types of guns that people could buy, meant a dramatic change in the regulatory landscape from that date until now. And even though the NRA was able to stymie public health gun research after 1995 and protect the gun industry from various consumer safety regulations with the help of George W. Bush,[18] the precedent that allowed the federal government to involve itself in the activities and behavior of gun owners was and is now firmly established in practice and law.

In addition to generating more political action and advocacy by the gun industry and its allies, the flurry of gun control legislation that occurred during Clinton's tenure prior to the 1994 Republican "revolution" also sparked the growth and activity of gun control advocacy behind which came gun control research. In the forefront of the gun control movement was Sarah Brady, wife of Jim Brady, whose reaction to her husband's wounding during the 1981 assassination attempt on Reagan took the form of immersing herself in gun control advocacy, first by joining a somewhat moribund group known as Handgun Control, then renaming and re-invigorating it as the Brady Campaign to Prevent Gun Violence.

Brady's effort to create the first, truly national gun control advocacy organization was aided by the fact that she was not only an active Republican who had worked for the RNC prior to her husband's affiliation with Reagan, but had experience in political campaigning and public relations. But the fact that she was a Republican and was married to another Republican who almost lost his life as the result of gun violence meant that the NRA had to give her a certain amount of wiggle room in terms of the degree to which she could not be directly confronted or challenged on personal terms. And, as I am going to explain a few pages forward, the NRA's attempt to energize its followers by casting gun control advocates in very personally unflattering terms only began to be noticeable after Jim and Sarah Brady began, in the 1990's, to withdraw from the political scene.

I said earlier that I was going to return to the gender issue, and here it is. Just as women are victims or perpetrators of violence to a very small degree when compared to men, so the NRA has never been able to find a high-profile female who was willing or able to advocate a pro-gun line. This is ironic and even somewhat amusing, given the fact that the gun industry, having largely run out of new customers on the male side of the ledger, has of recent times tried desperately to convince women that buying and owning a gun for self-defense is a good thing. But the marketing effort aimed at women has produced little tangible results. And while a few female media conservatives (Laura Ingraham, Emily Miller) have spoken out loudly for gun rights, it's largely because these women use the pro-gun platform as a way of augmenting their *own* audiences rather than building more support among women for the NRA. I have trained more than 2,000 people in the gun safety course that my state requires in order to apply for a license to purchase and carry a concealed gun. And while women constitute perhaps one-third of my students, most of them come to the class with their husbands or significant others because it's basically something to do. On the other hand, I have sold several thousand guns in my retail store since the NRA started going after female consumers during Obama's first term, and the women who have bought guns from me account sales-wise for maybe five percent. Unfortunately, the FBI told me that they do not collect reportable data on gender from background checks, but Garen Wintemute found a similar lack of women's interest in guns from state registration data that he studied covering recent California sales.[19]

On the other side of the fence, the gun control side, major advocacy initiatives continue to engage women in leadership roles. The first and most famous was Sarah Brady, whose activities are recounted above, and female-gender gun control advocates are now firmly established in the public arena, led by Shannon Watts, founder of Moms Demand Action for Gun Sense and former U.S. Representative Gabby Giffords, who was thrust into a high-profile role in the gun debate after she was shot and near-fatally wounded in 2011. The problem with both these and other gun-control advocacy organizations is that while Watts in particular has modeled her organizational approach after the Mothers Against Drunk Driving campaign of the 1980's, the internet is both a blessing and a curse for developing grass-roots movements, because on the one hand it cuts the costs and the time involved in mass communications (which was demonstrated with the remarkable use of Facebook by Watts' group), but it also tends to depress the degree to which people get involved in actual organizational activities, because digital communication replaces face-to-face contact and is a much cheaper way to reach out. Thus, while the Moms group claims to have 186,000 "likes" on its Facebook page, does this mean that the organization can really count on active (and financial) support from 186,000 people?

Nevertheless, to the degree that the internet is the major environment today for the birth, growth and development of advocacy activities, the fact that it first started being used for mass communication directly after the 1993-94 gun control battles in Washington has resulted in an increase in pro-gun and anti-gun opinion-making on both sides of the argument. In addition to the NRA, which remains the gold standard for all gun advocacy groups in terms of influence, membership and cash, the gun lobby also gets digital support from the National Shooting Sports Foundation (NSSF), which is the gun industry's lobbying organization, along with hundreds of blogs that carry commentary and opinion of supposed interest to the gun community. On the other side there are also a wealth of opinion-making web portals, many of whom are offshoots of advocacy groups and not-for-profits that have proliferated in and around Washington, seeking to influence legislation or legislators or both.

But the arena in which most of the critical arguments about guns have taken place is in the arena that is the subject of this book, namely, the scholarly arena. Because nothing is as important to the legislative process and the drafting and debating of laws than the application and influence of experts in the field that is covered by any particular law. And this is true whether we are talking about a bill to regulate banks, or insurance, or health, or guns. Most legislators do not know the ins and outs of every industry and activity over which the government has an involvement, nor would we expect our representatives to be expert in anything more than a few issues for which they have particular concern. We would never expect, for example, for a legislator who represents a farm community to understand the nuances of the inner-city housing market, nor would someone elected by the residents of a metropolitan area have any real understanding of how the soil bank operates. And for this reason our legislative system and our legislatures both at the state and federal levels are structured to analyze proposed legislation at a micro-level through hearings conducted by committees, and it is at the committee level that persons who will be directly impacted by the legislation get a chance to have their say, but it is also at the committee level that experts in that particular issue often hold sway.

And who are these experts? They are usually individuals who are recommended to the committee by legislators who sit on the committee themselves. And while no legislator wants to be connected to an expert who turns out to be a fool, particularly since most committee hearings are covered by the media, there is also considerable latitude given as a legislative courtesy to the credentials that are used to justify the expertise of individuals who testify as expert witnesses on this issue or that.

It was during the hearings that eventually spawned the Brady Bill in 1993 and the Assault Weapons Ban in 1994 that experts and expertise on gun violence first emerged which were used from then until now to bolster the competing (and conflicting) points of view. For the NRA, this took the form of arguing that guns made Americans safer from crime and that many Americans, in fact millions of Americans, used guns on a frequent basis to protect themselves from the threat of crime. The contrasting argument put forward by the gun control crowd was that guns increased the risk of injury and death, and rather than protecting us from crime, made crime more violent with higher levels of injuries and deaths.

These two positions on either side have remained the core of the gun argument from the 1990's until now. Both sides have refined their talking points somewhat, in the case of the NRA arguing for a wider acceptance of concealed-carry laws and the elimination of gun-free zones, in the case of gun control groups, limiting access to guns and tightening concealed-carry and ownership laws in general. Both sides justify their positions with research that was conducted or publicized for the most part around the gun debates in 1993 and 1994. Both sides have continued to promote, revise and extend this research over the intervening twenty years. And both sides are represented by experts, scholars in and out of academe, who appear regularly in public forums, media outlets and legislative hearings to answer queries about their work or promote one or the other points of view.

It should be noted, incidentally, that the scholars and researchers whose expertise is used to bolster the arguments on both sides have spent virtually no time discussing the 2nd Amendment, which is why I mentioned above that the interest in the 2nd Amendment rarely turns on what the amendment actually says. And that is because the 2008 Heller decision, while affirming the right of most, but not all of us to keep a gun in our home for self-defense, did not really give either side in the gun debate what they wanted to come out of the court. Proponents of gun control were hoping for a decision that would restrict civilian access to guns only on the narrowest of terms, i.e., membership in a law enforcement or military organization; pro-gun activists on the other hand wanted the right to "bear" arms to be extended to carrying a gun in the street. And while Scalia, who wrote the majority decision, seemed inclined to deny a widening of his personal defense interpretation to protect concealed-carry constitutionally, he also made it clear that both history and precedent could not support restricting private gun ownership only to membership in a military or paramilitary force.

So the argument about guns, their use and abuse, doesn't have much to do with the 2nd Amendment, but rather is based on what gun "experts" believe to be the impact of guns on everyday life. This is what I call the social utility argument about guns, and it is the core issue between the two competing points of view. Because the whole point of whether or not we should control access to small arms ultimately rests on whether they have a social utility or not. Small arms, particularly long guns, had an unquestioned social utility when people needed to use them for protection and game on the farm and the frontier. But as the rural-based society waned, the argument that guns retained their traditional social utility, by definition, disappeared. Which means that either a new argument for the value of guns has to be developed, or there's no good reason for them to be around at all.

What I intend to do in this book is present a very detailed examination of the research that has been used to either justify or negate the present-day social utility of guns; i.e., explain the competing arguments for and against private ownership of small arms. But before we get into those details, I want to make a more general point about the two arguments themselves. Because the truth of the matter is, that both sides are being somewhat disingenuous about what they hope to achieve. It's not what they argue which may or may not be true. It's the motives that lie behind their arguments which need to be understood.

Let's take the NRA, or what I call the pro-gun argument first. In May, 2014, the U.S. District Court issued a ruling in a case that had become known as Heller II. Following the original 2008 Heller decision, the District of Columbia had to enact a procedure that would allow D.C. residents to purchase and keep unlocked handguns in their homes. The process that residents had to follow may have *de jure* met the court's 2nd Amendment concerns, but *de facto* made it next to impossible for anyone living in D.C. to buy a handgun. Basically what the D.C. Metropolitan police did was to take New York's 1910 Sullivan Law, which allows but effectively negates concealed-carry within New York City, and then made it even more onerous, time-consuming and frustrating for law-abiding residents of D.C.

Having become something of a fixture at national gun shows, Heller upped his presence by suing again, claiming that the provisions of the new gun procedure effectively negated his 2nd Amendment right to keep a gun for self-defense, particularly a new twist in the D.C. law that also made it just as difficult to keep a shotgun or rifle in his home (D.C.'s previous law denied handgun ownership but permitted access to long guns). In support of Heller's lawsuit the NRA produced as its expert witness Professor Gary Kleck, whose comments about this lawsuit were cited in a different context at the beginning of this chapter's text. Kleck, about whose research I am going to devote the entire next chapter, no doubt helped the plaintiff's counsel draft the argument to support Heller's charge that the registration process denied his 2nd Amendment rights. And after reviewing specific parts of the new law that were deemed to be burdensome, the plaintiff then stated that the regulations did not meet the District's own goal of promoting public safety, because "criminals circumvent the process by purchasing guns on the street and bypassing registration altogether."[20] In response, the District Federal Court not only dismissed Heller's case "with prejudice" (a not-so-polite way of telling the plaintiff not to bring the case back into that court), but specifically found that following the plaintiff's logic would "render practically any gun laws unconstitutional."[21]

Guess what? That's *exactly* what the NRA wants. They can't say it outright because if they did, they wouldn't be able to buy their way into a single senator or congressman's office, no matter how pro-gun that particular politician happened to be. But the NRA doesn't want to cherry-pick between this law and that law; they want every law-abiding gun owner to decide for himself how to use his guns. And by tirelessly and endlessly promoting for the last twenty years the notion that there is no legal solution to gun violence because only "bad guys" misbehave with guns, they have inculcated an entire population of gun owners to believe the bizarre idea that gun laws shouldn't apply to them at all.

On the other side of the table, however, the gun control folks are also trying to obscure their real agenda by pretending that they "respect" the 2nd Amendment, even as they try to figure out ways to limit access to guns to the degree that the amendment would be effectively a useless exercise in constitutional rhetoric. Even President Obama remembers to mention his "support" for the 2nd Amendment whenever he gets pissed off and makes a snarky comment about our "failure" to deal with the issue of guns. But I really can't blame him for being both frustrated about the lack of legislative progress on gun control as well as for acting as if he is really concerned about 2nd Amendment guarantees. He knows that if he said what was really on his mind about this issue he'd just inflame the other side even more and nothing in this area would ever get done.

Let's be honest, folks. Gun control advocates wouldn't care if every gun was taken away, loaded on C5 Lockheed Galaxy transports and dumped out at sea. Oh yes, maybe the average gun owner could keep a shotgun around for the occasional duck hunt or even a high-powered hunting rifle to bag a trophy deer. But as for all those handguns that hold 16 rounds or those black rifles that look like M-16s? There's really no reason for any civilian to own one of those things and to hell with those Constitutional guarantees. And as for the NRA-inspired notion that disarming the civilian population is what led to Hitler and other dictatorial regimes (the NRA has, of late, referred to itself as America's first "civil rights" organization), the truth is that Hitler disarmed Jews and communists because he believed they were political threats to the Third Reich, not because Germany was suffering from drive-by shootings in the street.

So the desire of the NRA and gun owners in general to do away with all gun laws is neatly counterbalanced by the desire of the gun control folks to do away with all guns. Except neither side can come out and directly say what they really want, so instead they rely on researchers and media personalities to produce or promote studies that make the same argument but in a more subtle, somewhat more scholarly way. The problem with this research, however, is that neither side goes into it *tabula rasa*, so to speak. In other words, there's no blank slate. The research agenda of both the pro-gun and anti-gun advocates is to help advance the political goals of their respective positions; i.e., more versus less guns. And while this doesn't mean that the research should be discounted altogether or even in part, it does mean that even the most diligent and responsible research project may contain flaws in its method or design.[22]

The research that supports the NRA's desire to promote more guns and less (or no) laws covers two basic themes. First and foremost is the idea that guns protect us from crime. This research, which began to be promoted by the NRA during the 1993-94 national debates, is based largely on surveys designed to indicate the degree to which people used guns to defend themselves against what otherwise might have been crimes committed against them. Since the actual number of what the FBI calls justifiable homicides is extremely low and documented figures for justifiable woundings with guns simply can't be found, figuring out how many times guns were used to prevent the commission of a crime becomes a major issue in determining the social value of owning a gun.

Not surprisingly, as we will see, the research on what is called defensive gun use, or DGU, tends to correlate quite neatly with the researcher's basic political stance vis-à-vis guns. Scholars who favor less gun regulation tend to conduct DGU research which registers DGU's in the millions every year; scholars representing a more regulated approach to gun ownership find DGU rates to be much less. And while the scholars who conducted the research were, at times, willing to suggest that perhaps the results could not verified to the furthest degree, the promoters of gun ownership like the NRA were not bound to respect or even be concerned that this research was not necessarily compelling or complete. Not only did the idea that guns were being used to protect Americans from crime gain currency as a basic proposition of the gun lobby, but it was presumed and announced with equal certainty that anyone who questioned the validity of this research was simply attempting to thwart the agenda and goals of the NRA.

The second basic proposition which the NRA and the gun lobby advances to prove the value of gun ownership is that guns not only deter crime through direct use or threat of use (DGU), but also represent a mental factor which impels criminals to avoid committing crimes because the potential victim may be armed. This argument is based on research which finds a positive correlation between the number of people who are legally allowed to carry guns (also known as CCW) and a declining rate of crime in those jurisdictions. The two arguments supporting an armed citizenry are linked in terms of strategy by an ongoing campaign to get more guns into the hands of more people, which means less control over guns.

On the other side of the argument we also find two basic positions to justify more gun control and hence, less guns. Like the research whose results are used by the NRA, the gun control research also began to appear in the early 1990's, and was used to justify the gun control laws enacted in 1994-94. Here again there are two basic arguments that are linked together and have been the subjects of significant bodies of research. The first proposition is that the existence of so many guns does not make the US a more violent country than other Western countries, but makes our violence more deadly than anywhere else. The proof for this argument is based on comparing per capita firearm ownership with rates of violence and homicide, which results in similarities of the former but wide disparities of the latter. The second argument, connected to the first, is that access to guns on an individual basis does not make people safer, but results instead in higher rates of assaults, homicides and suicides perpetrated with guns.

So the running argument about whether we should or should not control guns gets down to trying to prove that the existence of guns results in certain social benefits or certain social costs, the benefits being protection from crime, the costs being greater levels of injury. I am going to spend the next three chapters analyzing and discussing each of these four arguments in detail, but before I move to that discussion, I want to make some general points which apply to both sides. When all is said and done, the argument about guns gets down to whether guns prevent or increase violence, and this is a particularly difficult problem because violence is a very complex behavioral phenomenon and, if it is violence that accompanies criminal activity, we are also introducing a second very complex problem—crime—which is also extremely difficult to analyze or understand. And bear in mind that while criminal use of firearms accounts for perhaps three-quarters of all gun-related injuries, we also have to confront the issue of guns used in suicide, which accounts for the remaining 25% of all gun injuries (and two-thirds of all gun deaths), which then introduces yet a third extremely complicated factor into the discussion, namely, the issue of mental status as it relates to depression.

There is also an enormous gap in the methodology that is used to create research protocols provoked by the fact that we can talk to some of the victims of gun violence but to virtually none of the perpetrators. Almost all of the perpetrators of suicide are dead, forty percent of the homicide perpetrators and less than thirty percent of the assault perpetrators are ever caught, and once they are in custody the legal issues surrounding their incarceration effectively rule them out as qualified research subjects. So at best we wind up either inferring causal relationships from indirect data, or making assumptions about behavior that led to the event only through analyzing information that is collected after the event.

Not only is it difficult to analyze the status of the perpetrator and the victim in many events involving guns, it's also difficult to understand the status of the gun, or what in forensic terms is called the "instrument." For example, we know that people who recently purchased guns are more prone to use them for suicide than people who did not. We also know that people have a higher suicide rate where a gun is in the house than people who do not own a gun. Both these studies link the impulsivity of suicide, which is generally understood, with the fact that the victims could easily and quickly get their hands on a gun. But this information is based on studies of suicides that take place in the home. Meanwhile, the suicide rate for people who shoot themselves away from their home is also higher than people who commit suicide outside the home using a method other than one involving a gun. But what we don't know is whether this latter group acted impulsively and quickly or did they travel around for a bit or did they always carry the gun when they went out anyway or what?

Not only don't we know how people behave once they decide to use a gun, we also don't know much about how they get or got their hands on a gun in the first place. It is assumed that most guns used in criminal assaults, robberies and homicides became the property of the perpetrator through one illegal channel or another, either because the shooter was too young to purchase a gun legally, or had a previous conviction for a violent crime which would prohibit them from owning or purchasing a gun legally. It is also presumed that most people who shoot themselves either intentionally or unintentionally were either the legal owner of the firearm that was used or could have acquired the gun through legal channels.

For the pro-gun lobby, more gun control will not prevent criminals from getting their hands on guns because, by definition, criminals don't obey laws anyway. For the people in favor of more gun controls, making it more difficult for everyone to get their hands on guns (through, more instance, purchase limits or global background checks) will result in less guns ending up within the criminal population, even though more controls will have little impact on the use of legally-acquired forearms in suicides, which is the single largest category of firearm fatality by far.

Despite the plethora of research generated over the last twenty-odd years, the assumptions by both sides about what will happen if guns are more or less available remain for the most part untested and unproven. This is not because of the lack of research per se, even though, as I will discuss in Chapter 5, The National Academy of Sciences found large gaps in our knowledge in 2002 and Obama's Commission to set priorities for new research found a similar lack of data in 2013. The reasons why so much of the gun argument remains within the purview of unsubstantiated rhetoric has to do with two things. First, as I mention above, it just doesn't seem likely that we can really understand the how's and the why's of gun violence given the difficulty of analyzing the behavior of the perpetrators. But there is a second reason that needs to be considered as well which flows from the assumptions that both sides make not about the social utility or social cost of guns, but the manner in which they view the outcome resulting from the success of the other side's agenda. And here I am going to borrow a schema from the brilliant political scientist Albert Hirschman, who published a small book on political theory that analyzed the rhetorical tradition of conservative responses to progressive social change from the French Revolution onwards;[23] an analysis which can be used profitably to understand the debate between conservatives versus progressives over the issue of guns.

Because while I have barely mentioned it, pro-gun and anti-gun lobbies share, among other things, a very clear adhesion to larger political forces, ideologies and political parties who use guns as a motif for advancing larger political agendas and political programs. Gun-rich states that contain the majority of privately-owned firearms in America tend to be red states located in the South, the West and the more rural areas of the Midwest. These are also the states with fewer gun laws and fewer Democrats. Blue states, on the other hand, tend to have less guns, more gun control, and fewer Republicans. Rarely, if ever, does the "gun issue" decide a statewide or even a congressional election because, for the most part, in red states or electoral districts everyone tends to be pro-gun, while in blue states and electoral districts support for gun ownership is softer on both sides of the aisle. While there are some places where the red-blue, pro-gun, anti-gun division is not so clear, exceptions such as Colorado generally prove this rule to be true. Colorado has a high degree of per capita gun ownership which is typical of Western states, but because of shifts in the state's demographic and ethnic makeup, it has also been the location of the most intense battleground for gun control over the last few years.

The scholarship that surrounds the gun debate is therefore not just of interest and concern for discussions about guns. It also tends to support or flow against positions taken by conservatives versus progressives on the wider scheme of things. Scholars who publish research that promotes the NRA position that more guns equals less crime also tend to publish works that promote other issues which align with the conservative point of view. Progressive scholars, on the other hand, who find that guns are hazards to our health, tend to subscribe to progressive notions about a wider role for government in regulating social and economic affairs.

But what is most interesting about the alignment between politics, policy and guns on both sides is the degree to which the pro-gun and the anti-gun proponents use exactly the same schema when advancing the argument for what would happen if the other side in the gun control debate was to win. And while Hirschman focused his analysis, for the most part, on conservative reactions to progressive social change, his analysis works just as well when we turn things around and look at how progressives view the results if the conservative position on gun control were to end up ahead.

Hirschman found that conservative reaction to progressive reforms has usually been couched in three anti-progressive arguments, or what Hirschman called theses: the "perversity thesis," the "futility thesis" and the "jeopardy thesis." The perversity thesis argues that any action taken to improve things will only make the existing situation worse. The futility thesis argues that the attempt to change things won't change things at all, and the jeopardy thesis argues that the cost of the reform is too high because it endangers or threatens a previous accomplishment.

The attempt by the NRA and the gun lobby to promote more gun ownership emphasizes the positive social value of guns, but also uses the perversity, futility and jeopardy theses to criticize the views and strategies of the anti-gun side. In other words, more gun control will only make it harder for "good guys" to get guns and therefore make us more vulnerable to the "bad guys" with the guns—the perversity thesis. Since "bad guys" don't obey laws, passing new gun laws won't result in less gun violence—the futility thesis. And finally, passing new laws will result in crime going up and therefore gun control will increase, not decrease the costs of gun violence—the jeopardy thesis.

As for the gun control (or elimination) lobby, they advocate the negative social cost of guns, but also use the perversity, futility and jeopardy theses to challenge the "more guns" position of the NRA. Ready? Loosening gun controls will result in more felons getting guns and, hence, more gun violence—the perversity thesis. Making it easier for children to get access to guns will result in more gun accidents—the futility thesis. Allowing more guns in civilian hands will not make us more violent per se, but will make our violence much more deadly—the jeopardy thesis.

This won't be the first time I've said it but I'll say it again: if the NRA didn't exist, Brady would have to invent it, and vice-versa. The problem with advocacy is that you go out of business pretty quickly if you don't have a target. But that doesn't mean the two sides are using arguments that are equally valid or based to the same degree on reliable data. It just means there are two sides. Which is what the great American gun argument is really all about.

CHAPTER 2

ENTER GARY KLECK AND PROTECTING OURSELVES WITH GUNS

In the mid-1960's, before guns were regulated by the Federal Government and the "gun issue" didn't exist, there were probably around 85 million privately owned guns floating around the United States, of which only 20 million were handguns. And of this total number, perhaps as many as two-thirds of the handguns had been manufactured before 1945, which meant that probably half of them didn't work.[1] Since the U.S. population in the mid-60's hovered around 200 million, this meant that maybe 5 percent of Americans at that time owned a handgun, in most cases some old revolver, a Smith or a Colt, probably manufactured before or after World War II.

Over the next thirty years, the national handgun stock increased to more than 80 million, which meant that on a per capita basis, handgun ownership increased from one out of twenty to one out of three and one-half. But not only did the per capita rate of handgun ownership triple between the Gun Control Act of 1968 and the Clinton gun bills of 1993-94, the character and caliber of the guns also changed dramatically during that same period. In the mid-60's most handguns were revolvers with capacities of six shots or less, and even though magnum-velocity ammunition had been developed in the mid-50's along with guns whose frames and cylinders could accommodate more powerful loads, most handguns were still chambered for older cartridges like 38 or 32.

This long-time revolver tradition that was part and parcel of our love affair with cowboys and the old West came to an abrupt end when the U.S. Army announced in 1979 that it was dropping an almost seventy-year reliance on John Browning's Colt 1911 pistol and replacing it with a double-action, hi-capacity gun chambered for the 9mm round. In fact, Smith & Wesson had been manufacturing such a pistol, the Model 59, since 1971, but the company's efforts to get the gun adopted by law enforcement or, for that matter, the civilian market, met with scant success. I purchased a Model 59 in 1978, and while I loved its black finish, sleek lines and 15-round magazine capacity, there was one little problem, namely, that the gun didn't work.

Well, it kind of worked. But it had a rather unique feature in that after slamming a loaded magazine into the gun while the slide was locked back from the last shot, sometimes in releasing the slide so that the gun would be ready to fire, the hammer also was released and the gun would then just go off. I still have a desk in my gun shop office which has a 9mm slug buried in the top panel when a Model 39, the single-stack version of the 59, performed in exactly the same fashion after I purchased it not so many years ago. As the gun discharged that little slogan from the gun industry ran through my head, "Once a piece of shit, always a piece of shit," but on another level I was happy to see that some traditions just don't give out.

In any case, until the Army announced that all the American-made guns that competed for the contract were rejected in favor of the Beretta 92, the fact that we were a revolver country and Europe was the place where everyone used pistols was just another example of American "exceptionalism," even if in this instance our unique style of gun engineering didn't quite measure up. However, to save some embarrassment in military circles, the Army's decision to outfit American troops with a non-American firearm was somewhat disguised by the requirement that the gun be manufactured over here. Which meant that even though the gun had been designed in Europe, to conform to ATF rules, the frame would be stamped "Made in U.S.A."

So Beretta showed up in 1980, built a factory outside of D.C. in Accokeek, Maryland, and then graciously gave a whole bunch of their pistols to the Maryland State Police. By the mid-80's, the virtual monopoly that Smith & Wesson had enjoyed on police sales had vanished, and by the early 90's with the appearance of Sig and Glock, the American handgun market increasingly relied on hi-powered, hi-capacity pistols that held 15, 16 or even 18 shots. So the stock of handguns in America was not only shifting from six-shot revolvers to hi-cap, semi-automatic pistols, but it was also shifting from long guns to handguns as well. In the early 60's for every handgun found in an American residence there were at least three long guns; by the 90's as many handguns as long guns were being manufactured by gun makers either in the U.S. or brought in from abroad.[2]

The shift from shotguns and rifles to handguns however, did not just reflect a change in buying tastes as European pistols became more popular and revolvers died out. It also was the result of a long and steady decline in the populations that traditionally favored long guns; i.e., rural residents, hunters and families living on farms. In 1900, more than half of all

Americans still lived in communities with less than 2,500 inhabitants, a percentage that shrunk to less than a quarter of the national population over the following fifty years. The suburbs also doubled in number of inhabitants during that same period, and would double again by the end of the last century.[3] Both of these trends—urbanization and absence of farming—meant a continued shrinkage of the gun market traditionally associated with long guns. What replaced this segment of the gun market was handguns, particularly pistols, which were increasingly the weapon of choice in non-rural zones.

But in order to expand the handgun market there had to be some consequent reason why this type of weapon was necessary to own at all. And this was not just an issue of market share as determined by the number of guns that were bought and sold, it also required a re-shaping of perceptions about the use and necessity of handguns because gun manufacturers needed to increase selling prices since long guns had traditionally sold at higher prices than pistols and revolvers. Hence, if the demand for guns shifted away from products that were traditionally more expensive to products with price points that were not as high, the only way to stay profitable was to increase the prices for handguns by making consumers believe that they were purchasing an item whose utility and necessity overcame the question of cost.

I had a great-uncle named Ben DeMain who, shortly after he arrived here from Eastern Europe in the 1920's, struck out for the North Carolina frontier, God only knows why. He ended up in Kinston where he opened a pickle factory, and then in the 1950's took a couple of rooms in the back of the warehouse where he started to manufacture guns. He called his gun company the Imperial Metal Products Company, and called his gun the IMP. It was a five-shot, 22-caliber revolver with plastic grips and a 2-inch barrel, what became known as a "Saturday Night Special" because it was small and cheap and could be easily concealed in your pocket in case things got noisy and rowdy in the saloon on Saturday night. The gun cost retail around twenty bucks; I think Ben turned them out for five dollars apiece. None of the internal parts were forged, they were all stamped, which meant the gun usually fell apart after it was fired once or twice.

The 1968 Gun Control Act put the Imperial Metal Products Company out of business because the law gave the ATF the right to set manufacturing standards for guns, particularly the tensile strength of the metal frame, which basically required the frame, the barrel and the cylinder to be forged rather than stamped. The whole point of this bureaucratic exercise was to drive manufacturers of "Saturday Night Specials" out of the market, the theory being that if gun prices increased, criminals and other low-class individuals would stop using guns, with a consequent decline in violent crime.[4] So much for another brilliant public policy move to cut back the criminal use of guns. My great-uncle Ben and other makers of the cheap guns went back to bottling pickles, cheaply-made guns disappeared, and in the aftermath of the 1968 Gun Control Act, gun crime went up.

And because crime started to increase for reasons having nothing to do with the cost of guns, the NRA found a ready-made argument for handgun sales, namely, as armed resistance to crime. The message started to appear in the 1980's, but really caught on with the beating in 1991 of Rodney King and the Los Angeles riots that erupted after the cops who were charged in his assault were acquitted in 1992. Following these events we then had the O.J. trial in 1995, and I don't believe there was a single American adult (or child, for that matter) who didn't watch one, two or all three of these events. And what was played out in all three instances were variations on the theme of black versus white, violence and crime. The fact that 90% of all violent crime, then and now, was intra-racial and not interracial was a reflection of the degree to which housing patterns in suburbs and cities were still and today remain largely segregated.[5] But reality and perception often don't coincide, and the perception of criminal danger generated by those media-spectacular events was heightened by a general crime wave in the early 90's fueled by crack cocaine which made even the most isolated and protected middle-class residents concerned about crime.

Enter Professor Gary Kleck and the idea of defensive use of guns. Kleck was hardly the first researcher who tried to analyze the social utility of firearm ownership based on the notion that having a gun meant that the owner could better protect himself from crime. And in fact, some of the first research that was used to bolster the contrary view, that the cost of gun violence had become excessively high, did not take into account the possibility that for every dollar spent to cover the costs of gun injuries and deaths, that perhaps even more money was saved because gun ownership prevented many crimes and therefore reduced the actual cost of crime.

Kleck's foray into the DGU world came in a long article published in a student-run law journal at Northwestern University.[6] I happen to be a graduate of Northwestern University, so you'll forgive me if I am less than ecstatic about the University's decision to support the publication of an academic journal which doesn't even pretend to engage in any kind of peer-review process before an article is accepted and goes to print. I say this because Kleck's article, as opposed to his earlier *Point Blank* book, is so unbalanced and so lacking in even a shred of objective analysis, that I wonder whether he was really of his right mind when he sat down and wrote the text out.

Perhaps the only unquestionably valid statement in the entire publication is the very first sentence where he states that "crime victims used to be ignored by criminologists." He then goes on to note that while some research on victims first appeared in the 1940's, it was in the 1970's that concerns about crime victims from a research perspective began to appear. What he doesn't say is that the turnabout in criminology towards a focus on crime victims was provoked most importantly by the decision of the Federal Government to create the National Crime Victimization Survey in 1973, whose findings on defensive gun use form the basic picture which Kleck would attempt to challenge and discredit in his own work. Except that what we will see is that previous to discovering the shortcomings of the NCVS surveys, Kleck himself used NCVS data to develop arguments about victim resistance to crime that he would later contradict in his work on DGUs. But before we discuss the interesting and largely unnoticed way in which Kleck has slithered back and forth between first accepting and then rejecting government data on how victims defend or don't defend themselves against crimes, I want to spend some time looking at the NCVS itself.

The survey is based on in-person interviews conducted by the Census Bureau twice each year with more than 160,000 persons living in more than 90,000 households.[7] This makes it by far the most extensive survey on crime conducted in the U.S. The purpose of the survey is to capture the true rate of criminal behavior and compensate for what has always been a tendency of crime victims to underreport criminal events. The fact that FBI-UCR and NCVS data differs widely in terms of numbers and rates of crime should not surprise because the information is not only compiled differently, but also covers different groups of victims and different types of crimes. The UCR draws its information from police agencies whereas the NCVS is based on a large sample of civilians. The UCR only counts crimes that each police agency counts as having occurred, even though definitions of crime occurrence (reported versus investigated) may differ widely from one agency to the next. In the case of the NCVS, persons who are surveyed are asked to talk about crimes whether or not they were reported to the police. Finally, the UCR counts all victims regardless of age; the NCVS does not engage respondents less than 12 years old, and the latter survey does not include homicides, whereas the homicide number may be the most accurate category of crime compiled by the UCR.[8]

What makes the data collected and analyzed by both the UCR and NCVS important, however, is the ability to see changes in the data from year to year. Both surveys attempt to maintain enough consistency in the methodologies they employ to generate data trends that can be consistent in terms of what they tell us about changes in crime over time. And generally speaking, the year-to-year trends of criminal activity from both sources tend to agree. Which is the single, biggest problem with the DGU survey conducted by Kleck, namely, that it was a one-shot, one-time only activity which, by definition, needs always to be judged with a great deal of care.

But Kleck wasn't interested in being careful, he was interested in establishing himself as someone whose work could show the social and cultural utility of gun ownership beyond what had traditionally been considered the traditional sporting use of guns. Kleck's research, after all, was published in the aftermath of the 1993-94 gun debates which, for the first time, saw the Federal Government instituting gun control measures aimed at reducing the use of guns in everyday criminal acts. And the debates that resulted in the Assault Weapons Ban and the Brady Bill took place simultaneously with an upsurge in violent crime, due largely to the crack-cocaine epidemic, which provoked a generalized fear of criminality and criminals armed with guns.

All of which put gun-owning organizations like the NRA on the defensive. But what if you could show that owning a gun was a good thing to do? What if you could show that the high levels of gun violence and homicides would have been significantly higher if average, ordinary people hadn't used guns to stop crimes? The problem was that the data that the government relied on to quantify the use of civilian-owned guns to stop crime didn't show the social utility of guns to be true. If anything, it showed that the number of times that citizens used guns to halt or thwart crimes was a small fraction, perhaps only 10 percent, of the number of times that people were victimized by guns. This didn't make a very good argument for more gun ownership, particularly handgun ownership, and it certainly didn't make a strong argument for the corollary of more handgun ownership, namely, an extension of laws that allowed the average citizen not just to purchase and own a handgun, but to walk around with it in his pocket or her pocketbook in a legal way.

Historically, gun ownership had always been part and parcel of America's traditions, but the ownership and use of handguns, as compared to rifles and shotguns, had always been more strictly regulated and controlled. It wasn't uncommon in the Old West for handguns to be restricted or banned altogether even in the wildest frontier towns.[9] And while though New York City's Sullivan Law enacted in 1910 was perhaps the most stringent of all handgun laws, if you were a New York City resident and wanted to purchase and keep a rifle or shotgun in your apartment, until recently the licensing process was straightforward, simple and didn't even require registering the specific gun.

But if more states and localities would allow legal concealed-carrying of handguns, this would not only make citizens more determined to undergo the licensing process for qualifying to own handguns, but would also counteract the gradual disappearance of long guns due to the general decline in hunting that was occurring as the United States increasingly became an urban and suburban society. By the mid-1980's, handguns were now more than 50% of all guns manufactured and imported into the United States, and the growth of the handgun market would be the engine for the gun industry's growth in the years that followed. In 1986 there were only 10 states that either had no or minimal restrictions on concealed-carry licensing; by 1995 it was 21 and by 2003 the residents of 36 states could be granted concealed-carry privileges without difficulty.[10]

Thank Gary Kleck, who routinely testifies before various Courts, legislators and Congress on gun control matters, and is usually paid $300-$350 per hour for his efforts on behalf of gun owners, gun dealers and the gun industry in general. But more importantly, it is his DGU study that is routinely offered up by virtually every anti-gun control media channel and organization to back up their claims about the damage that will be inflicted on the average American if we aren't allowed to walk around with guns. Here's a statement from the Cato Institute, one of the premiere conservative think-tanks, on the virtues and values of DGUs: "if harm reduction is the goal, policymakers should pause to consider how many crimes—murders, rapes, assaults, robberies—are thwarted by ordinary persons who were fortunate enough to have access to a gun. The bottom line is that gun owners stop a lot of criminal mayhem every year."[11] The real bottom line is that the Cato Institute, which occasionally pretends to base its advocacy on scholarly research, lifted this unvarnished statement directly from Gary Kleck.

It's not every day that the work of a single scholar has been able to produce such a windfall of public policies that fly in the face of evidence directly contrary to what that scholar claims to be true. And not only is the evidence that Kleck has produced on DGUs unreliable and, by any measure, simply wrong, but as I stated above, it's contradicted by other research published by Kleck himself. But before we look at contrary DGU arguments made by scholars including Kleck, let's first look closely at his own research on DGUs and see how well it holds up based on the arguments that he presents in the DGU research itself.

The data gathered by Kleck and published in 1995 was based on 4,977 "random" telephone interviews from which 213 respondents, or 4%, stated that they had engaged in a defensive gun use over the previous five years or within the past year. It was assumed that respondent's memories would be sharper if the event that they describe took place in the past year, but they were also asked about the five-year period to avoid problems which occur when survey respondents "telescope" their recall of any kind of event. The survey also made its overall DGU estimates based on first-person responses; i.e., the respondent had to be the individual who was involved in the DGU, rather than reporting on an incident that involved someone else.

Kleck begins an analysis of his findings by pronouncing that his survey is the "first survey ever devoted to the subject of armed self-defense."[12] But going into the study he's already decided that the only type of armed resistance that interests him is crime victims who defended themselves with guns. Even though there are many other weapons that people can use to arm themselves (knives, clubs, etc.), these options or others don't interest Kleck because there are no what he calls "policy implications" of defense against crimes other than guns. And what are the policy implications that concern Kleck? Here's where he gives himself away: "**any** form of gun control that disarms large numbers of prospective victims, either altogether, or only in certain times and places where victimization might occur, will carry significant social costs in terms of lost opportunities for self-protection."[13]

It's the phrase "lost opportunities for self-protection" that transformed Kleck's research into nothing more than shabby pandering to an industry looking for new marketing opportunities. Because from this time forward, the gun industry and its allies and supporters have wasted no opportunity to promote the notion that guns have a social utility that gives them in a unique, and indeed, unquestioned value. After all, who would argue that nothing is more important than the sacred duty to protect hearth and home?[14]

But since Kleck had to maintain certain scholarly pretensions in order to use this survey as the basis for remaining a member of the research-reliant academic club, so to speak, he needed to find a way to justify and validate his survey results which were so dramatically different from the data that had previously been accepted by scholars as representing the true nature and degree of armed resistance to crime. And chief among this data were the bi-annual surveys of the Justice Department, conducted for them by the Census Department and known as the National Criminal Victim Survey, or NCVS. The NCVS, as stated earlier, began producing information about criminal victimizations in the mid-70's, and continues to produce this information today. It is information from the NCVS, among other sources, which shows a steep decline in violent crime over the last twenty years, trends which the gun lobby announces with great glee to "prove" that as the country's arsenal of private weapons continues to grow, so the crime experienced by Americans continues to decline.[15]

But the value of the NCVS survey to the gun industry was much different when Kleck set out to create his DGU manifesto in 1995, because at that time the degree to which crime victims defended themselves with guns was, in the eyes of Kleck, absurdly low. In fact, there were substantially less than 100,000 DGU's each year according to the NCVS, which would hardly constitute enough anti-crime gun use to support any argument for gun ownership at all, never mind walking around with a concealed gun. But when you set out on a mission, as Kleck did, to create a scholarly justification for the positive social utility of guns, the first thing you need to do is convince your constituencies that any contrary arguments shouldn't be taken seriously at all. It's not just that your numbers are so different from the other side that makes your argument so powerful; it's that the way in which the opposition collected its numbers was simply wrong. Kleck's criticism of the NCVS data on the use of guns as a way to resist crime wanders around from here to there but ultimately focuses on one basic point, namely, that any numbers about gun use generated by a government agency must be suspect because people won't, as a rule, tell the government about ownership of guns. Since "guns are legally regulated, a victim's possession of the weapon, either in general or at the time of the

DGU, might itself be unlawful, either in fact or in the mind of a crime victim who used one." In other words, respondents usually could not mention their defensive use of a gun without, in effect, confessing to a crime to a federal government employee.[16]

Despite the fact that NCVS interviewers begin every interview with a clear statement about protection of privacy, and despite the fact that many of the NCVS questions could result in answers that a diligent prosecutor could utilize to initiate investigations into possible criminal behavior by the respondents to the survey (such as the questions and answers about who actually threw the first punch), Kleck knew that the audience and the market he was really trying to reach was, by definition, suspicious of any government-directed survey and thus would be amenable to assuming that the responses about DGUs in the NCVS was far too low. But Kleck's strongest objection to the data presented by the NVCS, which was completely and directly answered by the methodology of his own survey, was that the NCVS interviewers didn't undertake to find out about the use of guns for crime prevention in and of themselves; rather, they asked "only general questions about whether they did anything to protect themselves. In short, respondents are merely given the opportunity to volunteer the information that they have used a gun defensively."[17] As opposed to Kleck's survey in which the whole point of the interview was to elicit information about using guns as protections against crimes and nothing else.

In the interests of full disclosure, I must confess that until I checked the source that Kleck cites for the above statement, I wasn't really all that convinced that his research and conclusions were as full of holes as I will shortly attempt to show. But in fact the source he cites for stating that people interviewed by the NVCS were only asked "general" questions about protecting themselves comes from the actual interview questionnaire itself.[18] And what he says about this questionnaire is simply not true. Get it? Not true as in false. Not true as in making it up.

In fact, the NVCS questions about how victims protected themselves from crime are just as specific as the questions in Kleck's own survey; they go further and deeper into the specific circumstances of the criminal event itself; and if Kleck or his co-author read the NCVS questionnaire they are lying, or if the information was given to them by some third party they should have checked it out. But let me be a little more polite and withdraw the accusation that Kleck was lying; let's just say that he completely misstated and mischaracterized the NCVS report.

The questions about resistance to a criminal attack are found on the NCVS form known as the Crime Incidence Report. The report begins with a series of questions about where and when the incident occurred (in the home, the street, in daylight, at night, etc.). These questions are followed by a set of questions that ask the following: *Did the offender have a weapon such as a gun or knife, or something to use as a weapon, such as a bottle or wrench?*

If the answer to the above question was "yes," the respondent is then given the following choices: Hand gun (pistol, revolver, etc.); Other gun (rifle, shotgun, etc.); Knife; Other sharp object (scissors, ice pick, axe, etc.); Blunt object; other (specify).

This is followed by a lengthy series of questions detailing the type of attack and whether the victim was harmed in any manner and the degree of injury suffered either by the victim or to the victim's property.

Then comes the following question: *Did you do anything with the idea of protecting YOURSELF or your PROPERTY while the incident was going on?*

If the answer to that question was "yes," the respondent is then given the following choices, and can indicate positive responses to more than one response: (1) Used physical force towards offender; (2) Resisted or captured offender; (3) Scared or warned off offender; (4) Persuaded or appeased offender; (5) Escaped or got away; (6) Got help or gave alarm. And if the victim indicated that they responded by doing something in Category #1, they are then given the choice of indicating that they used a gun, a knife, another kind of weapon, or *threatened* to use a gun, knife or other weapon (my italics).

Not only does the NCVS ask specific and explicit questions about whether the victim was attacked and how the victim was attacked, but it also then gives the victim explicit options to describe the manner in which they attempted to resist the crime. Kleck's description of the NCVS and his reason for doubting its validity when compared to his own survey is because the NVCS "has been carefully refined and evaluated over the years to do as good a job as possible in getting people to report illegal things which *other* people have done *to* them."[19]

Wrong. The NCVS goes into much greater detail than Kleck's survey in allowing respondents to describe exactly the manner in which they resisted a criminal attack. But Kleck was after bigger game than simply figuring out how to prove that his survey based on 213 completed interviews was more valid than the NCVS survey based on interviews conducted with more than 45,000 respondents twice each year. Because as he said, his survey was the first one "ever devoted to the subject of armed self-defense."[20] But the question that really needs to be asked in order to decide whether Kleck's data should be taken as more valid than the information contained in the NCVS is this: what exactly were the people interviewed by Kleck defending themselves from?

The whole point of the NVCS is that it is based on testimonies from individuals who claim to have been the actual victims of a criminal event. Now maybe in some cases they didn't remember exactly what happened; maybe in other cases they made it all up because nothing happened at all. But either way, if a potential respondent reported that they had *not* been victimized by a crime, the interview did not take place. Kleck, on the other hand, wasn't looking for people who used guns to resist crime; in fact, the whole point of his survey was to interview people who used a gun not to defend themselves from a criminal attack, but to prevent a crime by letting someone who might have otherwise attacked them know that they had a gun.

I find this methodology very unique. You're not asking people about something that happened to them; you're asking them about something that might have happened to them whether there was any indication that what they believed was going to happen would actually have taken place. In fact, almost half the so-called attackers in Kleck's survey didn't threaten or attack the respondent at all![21] That being the case, how could Kleck even claim that his survey was designed to show resistance to crime or anything else? Last week I was sitting in my car in a parking lot in downtown Springfield, Massachusetts munching away on a breakfast burrito from a nearby Taco Bell. This parking lot is located about one-half mile from the intersection of Union and Orleans Streets which is the most favored spot in the Springfield ghetto for doing what seems to come naturally in that part of town, namely, getting shot. Last year there were 12 gun homicides in Springfield, of which 4 took place at this location, which means that while the gun homicide rate for the city as a whole is round 11 per 100,000 (four times the national rate), in the neighborhood of Union and Orleans it's around 70 per 100K.

As I was sitting in my car a young Hispanic guy came up to me with a cloth draped over his arm that obscured something he was holding in his hand. He began asking me for money, I put the car in gear and rolled away, the cloth dropped off his arm to reveal that he was holding an Android phone. I thought he was holding a gun. If my gun had been accessible would I have pulled it out rather than drive away? And if I had done so and then received a call from

Kleck's little survey company asking me if I had been involved in a DGU where a crime otherwise would have taken place, what do you think I would have said?

I knew two guys, customers in my gun shop, who reported that they used their guns in what I call non-criminal DGUs. Both incidents took place in lovely downtown Springfield, both men were white, both alleged criminals were black. In one case, the guy with the gun was stopped in his car behind another car when the driver ahead of him got out and began walking back towards him. He yanked the gun out of his belt, the driver of the other car retreated to his car and drove away. In the second incident the DGUer was about to stick his debit card into an ATM in downtown Springfield when a black guy came across the street and walked towards him. As the black guy got closer my gun shop customer turned and pointed towards the gun that was in his belt and the black guy turned and walked away. That was that.

Both of my store customers were not only sure that they had prevented themselves from being attacked, but they bragged about the incidents with great glee. In neither case was anything said by their alleged attackers, in neither case did their attackers brandish a weapon or in any other way indicate that they were going to commit a crime. But my two guys knew that they were in a high-crime neighborhood and they also knew that had they been unarmed they would have been attacked. The funny thing is that the guy in his car was stopped by the police a few blocks down from where the incident took place because the other driver, upon getting back in his car, got on his cellphone, called 911 and reported that someone was driving down Memorial Drive in a red Mustang and waving a gun. And even though my guy was then pulled over by the cops and asked why he had been seen waving around a gun, he knew that he had prevented a crime and he would have told Kleck the same thing.

What I am suggesting is that Kleck's interview method, in terms of generating valid data, strains common sense. But it also, according to other scholars, doesn't meet the most minimal academic criteria for evaluating or analyzing information gathered in a telephone poll, particularly information about what are considered "rare" events, such as protecting oneself from a possible criminal attack. This criticism was made most strongly by David Hemenway, who suggested in 1997 that even a slight misclassification of a response (citing it as an event that actually took place when, in fact, nothing took place; i.e., a "false positive"), could create a major overstatement of the incidence level of an event.[22] So, for example, if the actual incidence rate of an event is .2%, then 998 out of 1,000 respondents could possibly give you information that wasn't true and could be misclassified as a false positive, which if only 10 more people reported an event that took place when in fact it didn't take place, the resulting percentage increase would be 6 times higher, a statistical change that cannot be sustained in any serious discussion about survey sampling.

On the other hand, Kleck wasn't interested in a serious discussion; he was interested in elevating the social utility of guns to a level that previously had never been imagined. And Kleck's methodology with the resultant claim of 2.5 million DGUs annually provided much needed-ammunition for the gun lobby to counter studies which showed the annual cost of gun violence to be more than $100 billion in the 1990's, a number that has now increased to more than $170 billion.[23] On the other hand, if guns prevented 2.5 million serious crimes each year, this might have resulted in more than $200 billion in savings just from what otherwise would have been spent on medical response to injuries from rapes, robberies and aggravated assaults.[24] If Kleck had accepted the NVCS estimates for resistance to crime by using guns, it would be impossible to sustain the idea that the proliferation of guns, particularly handguns, was yielding positive results.

Yet while Kleck designed a survey methodology which upended what he considered to be the erroneous results published by the NCVS, it's interesting to note that he had no such qualms about using the same NCVS survey when it came to understanding whether resistance of any kind by a victim to a criminal attack would result in greater or lesser probability of injury to the victim himself. In 1993, Kleck co-authored a research paper based on NCVS data that studied victim resistance to robberies.[25] Using a sample of 4,500 robberies committed between 1979 and 1985, Kleck concluded that "when robbers had guns, victims who used guns for self-protection were substantially less likely to lose their property than other victims in general."[26] In other words, given the fact that guns are the most lethal form of self-protection (except perhaps a cyanide spray), guns are the most effective means of defense. But note what follows: "When victims faced robbers with any kind of weapons, victims using non-gun weapons were slightly more successful than those using guns, but armed victims in general did substantially better than unarmed victims."[27]

So Kleck now had two problems going forward if he wanted to show that guns had a positive social utility. On the one hand he had to find a way to promote the idea that guns would protect people from crime, even though his own study showed that there were alternate self-protection methods that worked just about as well. On the other hand he also had to reconcile the fact that the same data which he used to study self-protection from robberies also showed that very few people actually used guns to protect themselves from crimes. The answer? Announce that the data which you considered valid enough to analyze self-protection isn't really valid when it's used to analyze a specific type of self-protection—guns—because people won't admit to the government that they walk around armed. And just to make sure that your alternate evidence can't be compared to the data in NCVS, muddy the whole thing by claiming that you aren't interested in finding out whether guns are an effective means to protect people from crime, but whether guns are an effective means to protect people from *what otherwise might have been a crime* [my italics].

I must confess that I am astonished that anyone has ever taken such crap seriously. How can you create a valid survey that asks people to tell you what they think someone else was going to do when the person they are talking about gave no indication, either verbally or physically, that they were going to do anything at all? It would be like calling someone up and asking them not who they were going to vote in an upcoming election, but asking them to tell you how their next-door neighbor was going to vote, even if they had never talked to their neighbor about the election or about the neighbor's political beliefs or preferences at all. And yet, the notion that each year armed citizens keep millions of crimes from taking place, a notion based on Kleck's survey and nothing else, is consciously promoted by conservative think tanks like the Cato Institute, law enforcement professionals like the current Chief of Police in Detroit and, it goes without saying, the gun lobby itself.[28]

Even some of the most distinguished academic researchers who publish in related fields have come to the defense of Kleck's work, most notably the late Marvin Wolfgang, who may have been the leading criminologist in the United States and published a comment about Kleck's survey and noted that the work was correct because there was no "contrary evidence."[29] This is basically the same point made by the National Academies of Science which conducted a very thorough review of the Kleck survey in 2002 and, while it found significant gaps in the methodology, also concluded that the focus on respondents who perceived the possibility that they might be victims of crime meant that contrary evidence from the NCVS, which was based on persons reporting actual criminal attacks, did not invalidate the findings in Kleck's work.[30]

The problem with the National Academy of Science review of Kleck's research, and other academic critics, for that matter, is that the analysis of Kleck doesn't focus on the assumptions of his work per se, but rather they are based on comparisons of the different analytical methodologies that flow from whether the survey respondents were criminal victims, a la the NCVS, or whether they were just random, ordinary people standing on their porch or walking down the street who happened to have a gun in their pocket when someone walked up to them and maybe was going to engage in a criminal attack against them. What should we call people like that? They aren't crime victims because a crime never occurred. They also aren't gun owners because none of them were ever asked to explain how it was that they were walking around with a gun. For someone who based his entire criticism of the NCVS survey methodology on the alleged reluctance of people to tell a true and complete story to a government representative, Kleck must have assumed that he could trust the responses of his survey subjects to be honest and truthful because they weren't talking to a government official. I say this because there was absolutely no effort made to validate whether anything that was being reported was true; no witnesses, no police report, no nothing. But Kleck states again and again that his information is valid and the NCVS is invalid simply because of the identity of the interviewer. And academics like the National Academy take such nonsense seriously? But let's continue further and see if we can figure out a method to validate Kleck's results.

The most important question that has never arisen, as far as I can tell, in any of the critiques of Kleck, is the issue of options. It seems to me that if someone wants to make a serious argument for the positive social utility of guns as a means of self-protection, then at the very least one has to weigh the costs and benefits of self-protection with a gun against other types of self-protection. I mentioned above that Kleck actually used such an approach in 1991 when he analyzed the outcomes of robberies when the victim used different methods to prevent the crime from taking place. He did the same thing again when he studied resistance to rape in a paper he submitted to the Department of Justice in 2005.[31] In this latter study he looked at more than 14,000 sexual assaults, including more than 700 rapes, that were reported to the NCVS between 1992 and 2002. And much like the conclusions that Kleck drew from studying victim resistance to robberies, Kleck discovered that guns were no more helpful in preventing rapes than other forms of resistance, including "running away" and "calling the police."

But here we go again, because just as in the earlier paper based on NCVS data, Kleck cautioned that survey respondents would probably underreport gun use because the interviewer would have been perceived as someone with whom such information should never be shared. You would think that if Kleck were really interested in objectively analyzing the social utility of guns that he would have constructed and conducted a privately-based survey in which people were randomly contacted and asked to report how they protected themselves from a crime which actually occurred. If Kleck is so convinced of the honesty of his respondents in answering questions about how they behaved even if they didn't know that a crime was going to take place, why would they be less honest in describing how they reacted to an actual criminal event? I'll tell you why. Because in order to conduct research that might result in an honest understanding of the role of guns in crime or, for that matter in anything else, the first and foremost requirement is to try and find out how many people are actually walking around with guns. If you don't have some valid idea about that number, then there is simply no way that you can tell whether the incident you are researching is a rare event or not. And for all the talk about the social utility of guns, either from a positive or negative perspective, how come nobody has ever tried to figure out whether and how often the damn things are being used for anything at all?

For example, we know that roughly 15 million people purchased hunting licenses last year.[32] We also know from industry estimates that the average American hunter goes hunting roughly 10 times each year.[33] Which means that, in total, hunting guns are used 150 million times each year or 410,000 times per day. Now we know that hunting tends to be a fall activity and that most hunters go after small or medium game which is more readily available in certain parts of the country than in others. So on a given day there might be 600,000 people walking around with hunting guns in certain parts of the country and far fewer hunting guns encountered in other parts. But you get my drift, right? Of course I am relying on data gathered from people who hunt legally; i.e., they purchase a hunting license and probably also are carrying a legal gun.

When we get into the issue of carrying handguns, however, the ability to figure out how many guns are being carried for self-protection begins to fade. At least this is what Kleck has stated again and again as his rationale for not accepting the much lower estimates of armed self-protection generated by the NVCS. But Kleck's study, remember, was conducted in the early 90's when concealed-carry licenses were not as prevalent as they are today. In fact, in 1990 there were only 16 states that allowed for residents to secure concealed-carry licenses on a "shall issue" basis (i.e., if you applied for it you generally got it), while today just about every state grants some degree of concealed-carry privilege based on the same criteria that is used to determine whether a resident can purchase or own a gun at all.[34] So while the Supreme Court's 2008 Heller decision held that private gun ownership was a Constitutional "right" that did not require membership in a military or law-enforcement organization, this "right" only covered keeping guns in the home, but *de facto* the right has been extended to concealed-carry as well.

As of the beginning of 2012, there were 8 million active concealed-carry permits held by people living throughout the United States.[35] Now it's true that these 8 million concealed-carry permits vary in number from state to state and even within states depending on different rules for different localities, such as in New York where, generally speaking, it's much easier to get a concealed-carry permit in a rural, upstate county than in New York City where such permits are rarely granted to anyone other than security guards and the retired cops who guard Donald Trump. But if Kleck were to do his 1995 survey today, it would be pretty difficult for him to hold to the notion that a random cross-section of American adults would be unwilling to divulge whether or not they carried a gun because it just isn't something that needs to be kept secret, unless you were planning to do something illegal with the gun in the first place or were someone who did not have the legal right to carry a gun. And in a random telephone survey, the number of people who would fall into either of those latter categories today would be far outweighed by the number of people who could or would be walking around with a gun.

But nobody, as far as I know, has ever conducted a survey to determine how many people really are walking around armed, so I decided to do it myself; i.e., I sent out an email survey to 655 people who have been in the required gun safety course over the past 12 months that I teach based on the NRA Basic Pistol curriculum that is accepted by my state, Massachusetts, as a pre-requisite for the LTC. Massachusetts requires everyone who applies for a gun license to take this course, but the license itself both allows a resident to purchase and own guns, as well as to carry a concealed handgun without any additional licensing requirements. Some police chiefs, particularly in the larger cities, make applicants jump through additional hoops to get concealed-carry privilege, but in my part of the state an automatic CCW approval is usually guaranteed.

So I sent an email out to these folks and asked them two questions: (1) Had they applied and received their LTC and, if so, (2) How often were they carrying a gun? If they answered the first question in the affirmative, they then had five choices for answering the second question about the frequency of carry: always, frequently, sometimes, infrequently and never. I received 130 replies of whom 110 told me they now had the LTC. Of those 110 licensees, 11 said they carried all the time, another 15 said they carried frequently, and the remainder said they sometimes carried (26), infrequently carried (21) or never carried (37). And some of the people who said they carried a gun sometimes stated that they carried a gun for hunting or to go to the range.

I didn't explain why I was conducting the poll because I didn't want to bias people's answers one way or the other. But the bottom line is that of 110 people who had the legal right to carry a gun for self-defense, roughly 25% said they did so, and only 10% of the respondents carried a concealed weapon all the time. Now let's take these numbers and extrapolate against national CCW to estimate how many Americans go walking around with a gun to protect themselves each and every day. If there are eight million legal concealed-carry permits floating around, this means that something like 800,000 licensed CCW-holders are using a gun all the time to protect themselves against crime. But here's where things get a little sticky. Because roughly one-third of Kleck's respondents claimed that their DGU took place within their home. Which means that many of my respondents, including many who stated that they never carried a gun around, still could have used their gun to defend themselves from a crime.

So let's eliminate that part of the sample and just examine the data on using guns for self-protection outside the home. Since Kleck puts the total annual DGU number at somewhere above 2.5 million, we can thus say that roughly 1.8 million of these DGUs occurred in some location where the DGUer had to tote the gun. And if 800,000 or even one million people who have legal CCW carry their weapon with them all the time, each one of them would have to engage in a defensive use of the gun at least two times each year. I do not believe, incidentally, that Kleck interviewed a single respondent who claimed to have been involved in multiple DGUs. Which means that if the survey I conducted was at all representative of the gun-carrying habits of people with CCW, that people who carry a gun to protect themselves must be carrying out an awful lot of protection with that gun.

But wait a minute, you say. Even if there are more than 8 million valid LTC permits in the US, there are still lots of people who don't have the absolute legal right to carry a gun and if the government asks them about their propensity to use a gun for self-defense they are going to say "no." That may be true, but their presence in a survey alongside the ones who have CCW won't be such a significant factor because, believe it or not, the 10% of my respondents who said they carried a gun with them all the time represents the high-watermark of legal gun carriers with whom, had I conducted my poll with the same people a year later, the percentage who would have claimed they were still carrying their pieces probably would have dropped to 5% or even less.

Why? Because recall that I sent my email survey to people who had recently received their LTC. The ones who wanted to carry a gun went right out and bought a gun. And if they were "serious" about self-defense they didn't buy some cheap, used piece of shit. They bought a brand new Sig, or a Colt, or something else that cost seven, eight or nine-hundred bucks. After all, they had been dreaming about the day they could hook up their ninety-dollar, tactical/concealable holster and stuff it full with a real, live gun. Even the street criminals, who start carrying crummy little guns when they are in their teens, graduate to higher-priced, more quality merchandise when they come of age.[36]

Then know what happens? After a while, usually within the first year, the thrill wears off. There aren't that many gunfights out there anyhow, the gun is heavy and bulky as hell, and it's pretty tough to walk around on the beach flexing your biceps and somehow conceal your gun. Then finally, one night you're getting into the car to take the wife out to dinner or go visit friends and you remember that you forgot to strap on the gun. And you think, to hell with it, because you know that if you turn off the ignition and tell the old lady that you "forgot" something in the house, she's going to say, "Honey, do you really have to take that goddamn thing with you everywhere we go?" Or worse, you leave the gun out at night next to the bed and one morning you oversleep, throw on your clothes, go bolting out the door, get halfway to work and—*shit!*—the damn gun is sitting out next to the bed and the cleaning lady is due to let herself into the house at 10 o'clock. So you turn around, drive like mad back home, tear into the house, throw the goddamn gun into the safe and now try to figure out how to explain to the Vice President why you are late for the meeting, because if you tell him (or better yet, her) that you had to go back to secure your gun, you can kiss that year's bonus goodbye.

So the spell is broken. And that wonderful, beautiful new gun that's so much fun to tote around (and the biggest part of the thrill is the fact that nobody else knows that you are carrying it) is no longer fun, it's no longer something you like or want to do, it's something that has become a pain in the ass. Want to know how many customers have come into my store, proudly announced that they were buying their first "carry" gun, and then come back six months later to trade the gun in for a riot shotgun which is a much better weapon to use in defending hearth and home? Plenty. And I can tell from looking at (and smelling) the gun that it hasn't been shot at all. In fact, they often bring back the unused box of shells that they got when they purchased the gun. I'm not saying that this is what happens in most cases when people buy a gun for self-defense. I'm not even saying that it's true in many cases. But what I am saying is that the longer people own guns, the less frequently they will carry them. Which means that those 800,000 to 1 million who are walking around protecting the rest of us from the criminal element aren't even close to that number if we could actually figure out exactly how many people with CCW were engaged in defending the lives of ourselves and our loved ones each day. And this population is going to be involved in 2-3 DGUs every year in order to meet Kleck's estimate of two to three millions DGUs that allegedly take place? Give me a break Gary, will you?

What I find most interesting in the DGU debate is that it's understandable that the scholars who dismiss Kleck's crazy numbers could be accused, as they are accused of all the time, of not "understanding" the gun culture and therefore unwilling or unable to accept the fact that many law-abiding Americans walk around carrying a gun. But nobody on either side of the gun debate ever stops to imagine that maybe the champions of concealed-carry like Gary Kleck and others have no greater degree of knowledge about the gun "culture," and therefore promote notions about how, when and why people carry guns that simply are not true. Or to be more precise, it's not that what Kleck and others say that isn't necessarily untrue. It's that what they say may have something to do with views about life, about culture, about politics and society in general but it has little, if anything, to do with guns.

CHAPTER 3

ENTER JOHN LOTT AND THE VIRTUES AND VALUES OF CCW

Once Gary Kleck convinced the gun lobby that they could make an argument for the positive social utility of guns through the commission each year of millions of DGUs, it didn't take long for the other shoe to drop through promoting the idea that carrying a gun around legally was a good thing to do. Because the problem with Kleck's DGU study was that he never took the trouble to find out whether his respondents were legally allowed to actually walk around with a gun or even have one in their home. And it was the possibility that most people who used guns to protect themselves from criminals were not, indeed, supposed to have access to a gun, which formed Kleck's basic criticism of government numbers of DGUs. These government-derived numbers were much lower, often twenty times lower than Kleck's estimates, because people would never admit to a government employee that they actually had a gun.

On the other hand, if you could show that gun ownership was a factor in resisting and keeping down crime, then all the more reason to make it easier from a legal standpoint not only to own a gun but to carry it around. And at the same time that Kleck's work appeared, the NRA and local organizations of gun owners were in the process of transforming that part of the American legal landscape which enclosed and defined the ability of law-abiding citizens to walk around protecting themselves with guns. In 1985, ten years before Kleck's DGU study appeared, law codes in 33 states contained some kind of procedure that allowed residents to apply for and receive permission to carry a concealed weapon outside the home, even though 2nd-Amendment rulings to that date were still ambiguous about whether civilians not attached to some kind of military or law enforcement unit had the right to own guns at all.[1]

However, of the 35 states that issued concealed-carry permits, a majority of them, twenty, required that the applicant prove specific need, either for reasons of business, such as carrying around large amounts of cash or other personal circumstances, that necessitated a higher level of protection than what could be provided by the local cops. Many of the states that imposed special requirements for concealed-carry did not actually require licensing as a prerequisite for buying or owning a gun. I lived in South Carolina, for example, between 1976 and 1980, and the only documentation I needed to present to purchase a handgun was a valid driver's license, and while I had to fill out a Form 4473 and attest that I was not a felon, a fugitive or other type of disqualified person, the dealer did not check the answers on my form with anyone to see if I was telling the truth. On the other hand, getting a permit to carry a concealed handgun required an interview with the town magistrate and it helped if he not only knew me on a first-hand basis, but knew my family as well. The concealed-carry permit in South Carolina actually made its bearer a member of the state constabulary which, in theory, could be called out in moments of emergency to back up the National Guard. P.S., nobody could remember any time when this law-enforcement body was ever assembled for any purpose whatsoever.

The informal and rather personalized nature for granting concealed-carry privileges in South Carolina was fairly typical of what went on in most states that imposed some kind of specific licensing process in order to walk around with a gun. I should add that carrying a gun in your car usually did not require a permit, because in most states your vehicle was considered an extension of your home. But even in the minority of states that issued CCW (concealed-carry of a weapon) without requirements beyond the legal test for ownership of guns, there were often arbitrary and sometimes silly procedures that could be invoked if the issuing authority, the town chief or the county sheriff, decided to impose additional rules. And when such rules were, on occasion, challenged in the courts, the arbitrariness of the licensing authority was routinely upheld because gun ownership was a question of public safety and police were, after all, the final arbiters of what constituted public safety in their respective jurisdictions.

Back in the 1970's there was one county in South Carolina where the Sheriff couldn't read or write. He was a nice guy, spent most mornings in the local Hardee's down the road from his office, and routinely conducted interviews for concealed-carry licenses over a cup of coffee and a sausage biscuit before going out to his car, lying down in the back seat and taking a nap. Anything having to do with paperwork was handled by his "boy," a black man of indeterminate age but certainly older than the Sheriff, who had served some years of a murder sentence before he was paroled and took over running the county's law enforcement affairs. If you were a resident of this particular county you applied for a concealed-carry permit by sitting down with the Sheriff and reminding him that your cousin was kin to his niece or some other family connection like that, at which point the Sheriff would instruct his boy to "rustle up" one of those permit forms when he had a chance, fill it out and hand it over to you, and that was the end of that.

Along with the degree to which the issuance of concealed-carry licenses were subject to local caprice and whim, it was also the case in 1985 that 16 states had no licensing for concealed-carry (and one state, Vermont, from then until now, had no state law governing gun ownership at all). Many of the Western states permitted open carry of rifles and shotguns and some of them extended the open carry doctrine to cover handguns as well, particularly in parts of the state that were mostly open range and were still often worked by men riding horses, even if the horses had combustible engines and four wheels. But generally speaking, concealed-carry of handguns was not the usual kind of thing, nor before the mid-80's was there any real demand for change.

As I pointed out in Chapter 2, until the mid-1980's the civilian gun arsenal was comprised primarily of long guns; i.e., shotguns and rifles, and most, if not virtually all of the privately-owned long guns were used for hunting and outdoor sports. It wasn't uncommon, for example, to walk into a hardware store in farm towns or even large cities in the gun belt and find a long rack of rifles and shotguns against a wall, and a few handguns plopped in a glass case that also held watches or other ornamental doodads like electric egg-timers and crap like that. Behind the handgun case there was probably some handgun ammunition in various calibers and maybe a few leather holsters scattered here and there. And even though hi-capacity, European pistols were coming into the country and the Army was taking shipments of Berettas to supplant the venerable Colt 45, names like Sig and, in particular Glock were hardly household words. I saw my first Glock at a gun show in Kingston, New York in 1982 or '83 when one of my buddies, a NYPD veteran named Jack Clark, persuaded me to trade a Smith & Wesson Model 58 revolver in 41 Magnum for the damn thing, which Jack then bought from me for two hundred bucks. The joke was on him, however, because when he took the gun up to the licensing division to register it on his permit, he was informed that it could not be kept within the city limits (Jackie lived on Staten Island) because the NYPD, in its wisdom, had decided to ban personal ownership of Glocks since "plastic guns" could be taken through metal detectors in courthouses and therefore were considered a security risk.

That was the state of handgun ownership around the country in the mid-80's, which largely accounts for the lack of interest in CCW prior to that date. But the landscape then began to change rapidly as can be seen from the following graph:[2]

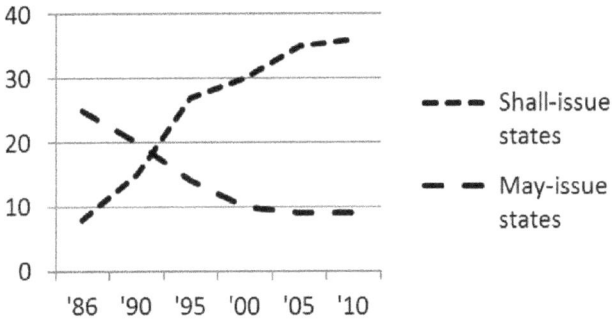

If we assume that "may issue" means more regulation and "shall-issue" means less, I cannot think of another consumer product that has undergone such a shift in regulatory controls over a corresponding period of time. From the way the NRA talks today about the dangers of gun control, you would think it would be the other way around. But what this graph makes clear is that not only do Americans have free access to firearms far beyond the access granted to citizens of any other Western country, but this access has become much greater and much less regulated over the past twenty-five years.

And even though the 2008 Heller decision declared that the 2nd Amendment gave Americans the *de jure* right to keep a gun for self-protection in their homes, *de facto* this right has been extended to the street due to the persistence and strength of the CCW movement throughout the United States.

Effectively, the shift from "may" to "shall" means that individuals can carry a concealed handgun on their person by dint of meeting the same legal qualifications that are accepted for purchase or ownership of firearms kept in the home; namely, the lack of legally-disqualifying circumstances like a felony charge, being a fugitive, a mental case, having renounced one's citizenship or a few additional things that hardly apply to anyone at all. Many but certainly not a majority of "shall-issue" states require some sort of pre-licensing training, but such training usually requires nothing more than being able to prove that you can hit the broad side of a barn. My state, Massachusetts, allows CCW with a safety course that doesn't require live-fire at all. Other states, like Florida, require a live-fire exercise but do not specify how many rounds must actually be discharged from the candidate's gun, and there are CCW courses in the Gunshine State that meet the training requirement after the applicant has shot his or her gun exactly once.

I cannot say with certainty why gun owners shifted their preferences from long guns to handguns over the last thirty years. Some of it had to do, no doubt, with a shift in consumer tastes involving polymer, MIM technology and miniaturization that has moved into every gadget field; nor can one discount the general decline in hunting and all outdoor sports, particularly those that require physical locomotion beyond getting in and out of a car or sport truck. Not that certain outdoor sports don't attract people who want to hike, kayak, backpack and the like; but that's not, generally speaking, the gun population, at least not yet. The truth is that people who want to be able to carry concealed guns around aren't doing it because they necessarily want to do something with the gun. It seems to be more in line with a general attitude towards security and safety in which carrying a concealed gun plays an increasingly important role in general attitudes towards guns.

Until the 1980's, most surveys of gun owners showed that ownership of guns was tied to their utility as hunting weapons or for general use around the farm. Keeping a gun for self-protection was always mentioned as a reason for ownership, but it usually was mentioned less than half as frequently as using a gun for work or sport.[3] The advance of self-protection and the receding of sporting/working uses in surveys of gun owners became noticeable around the same time that a spike in violent crime rates due to crack cocaine became the stuff of everyday and continuous media coverage both in print and on TV.

In the previous chapter I discussed how the public concern about crime and violence made people receptive to Gary Kleck's argument for the social utility of guns based on his discovery of millions, rather than thousands of yearly DGUs. But Kleck, as I pointed out, not only made no effort to determine whether his respondents were carrying the guns they used in DGUs legally, but argued that even his numbers were probably underreported because people wouldn't admit to doing something—walking around with a concealed gun—that they were not legally allowed to do. So if you want to believe that guns really do have a social utility by dint of being able to be used to protect us from crime, even from crime that may or may not actually take place, the answer is to make concealed-carry legal and therefore remove any impediment to being able to use guns as a means of self-defense.

Enter John Lott. In 1998 Lott published a book entitled *More Gun, Less Crime*,[4] which purported to prove that the extension of concealed-carry laws resulted in less crime. By 1995, the number of states that allowed some degree of CCW had grown from

24 to 42, and while Lott never distinguished between varying degrees of legal CCW ("shall" versus "may" laws), he explicitly tied decreases in crime rates both to the extension of concealed-carry laws as well as ownership of guns in general. Quoting Lott: "Allowing citizens to carry concealed handguns reduces violent crimes, and the reductions coincide very closely with the number of concealed handgun permits issued." [5] Thus Lott's work took Kleck to the next level of social utility, arguing that carrying a gun not only protected the individual himself from becoming a victim of crime, but made the larger society safer from crime as well.

Lott's argument gained a lot of traction after the Sandy Hook massacre, when the NRA called for armed guards in schools as well as an overall eclipse of what is known as "gun-free" zones. In fact, schools were defined as gun-free zones in a 1990 federal crime bill which prohibited anyone from brining a gun within 1,000 feet of any educational institution unless specifically authorized to be armed by state or local authorities. Although the bill was struck down by the Supreme Court for reasons having to do with the wording of the commerce clause in the legislation, it was re-instituted with more appropriate wording in 1996 and subsequent challenges have been unavailing.[6] The notion of gun-free zones also pervades many of the expanded CCW laws insofar as local and state governments have the discretion, often applied, to limit CCW in what they consider to be sensitive areas like schools, amusement parks and locations where liquor is served or sold. In certain instances and some jurisdictions the pro-gun lobby has been successful in pushing back on these gun-free limitations, but they have never been able to challenge the authority both of government jurisdictions and private companies to restrict or completely ban firearms from certain locations.

In July 2014 there were two significant instances in which the ability to limit CCW in certain locations was headline news; the first in Georgia where a new law widened the definition of physical locations where gun-owners could bring concealed weapons, and the second the decision by the Target store chain to make their retail locations as gun-free as possible. I'm going to talk about both of those situations before I get back to the CCW arguments made by John Lott.

In Georgia, a new law took effect on July 1, 2014, which wiped out most of the gun-free zones that had previously existed under statute throughout the state. This included any public facility that served alcohol, any church or other religious facility, many educational facilities and many government buildings. The law was vigorously promoted by the NRA and local gun organizations, just as it was decried as a major threat to safety and security by the gun control lobby. In fact, the law actually didn't change much in the way of widening gun-free zones for the simple reason that any facility, be it a church, a restaurant, a school, or what have you, could opt out of the gun-free status and simply declare itself not to be a gun-free zone. In effect, the law allowed people to carry a concealed weapon where previously they had not been allowed to do so, but only with the approval of the owner of a particular facility. And Georgia, which is listed in the Congressional Research Report on CCW as a "shall issue" state, still allows local judges, acting as the "issuing authority," to deny a concealed-carry permit to someone whom they feel does not have "good moral character" even if the applicant meets the legal guidelines for CCW.

The second interesting development in CCW also occurred in July, when the retail chain Target issued a corporate statement requesting, but not requiring customers to leave all concealed weapons outside of their stores. This action was taken because a group of publicity-hungry gun owners in Texas had marched into a Target store, as well as several other chain stores with assault-style rifles slung over their backs, using this particular type of guerrilla theater to publicize their demand that Texas once again revert to an old law that allowed for carrying weapons in open view. Target then found itself in the cross-hairs of a battle between the gun control movement, led by Michael Bloomberg's *Everytown* group, versus the anti-gun control advocates, most of whom weren't all that crazy about publicly supporting open displays of assault rifles anyway.

One thing led to another, the national media picked up and ran with the story for a couple of days, and the corporate management of Target felt obliged to issue a request—not a demand—that gun owners leave their guns at home. The statement was couched in conciliatory tones for both sides, noting that Target would not establish any store policy that ran counter to local or state ordinances on what people could or couldn't do, but it emphasized that Target was a family destination and that its family atmosphere might not be conducive to public displays of guns. This statement was not dissimilar to a please-keep-your-guns-out-of-our-stores statement issued several months previously by Starbucks, and in both instances a few internet mumbles on gun blogs about "boycotting" Starbucks and Target turned into nothing at all.

Now here's the point about both these stories. Notwithstanding the promotion of the social utility of guns through the effort to expand CCW and diminish both the physical and legal extent of gun-free zones, with the exception of Vermont, the United States still does not permit the unfettered ownership or carry of weapons by civilians in any jurisdiction whatsoever. Further, there is no state that either removes the arbitrary authority to issue permits for gun ownership and/or CCW, or denies private owners of public facilities the right to advise if not formally forbid weapons on their property. The distinction between "shall issue" and "may issue" of CCW, for example, is an exercise in uselessness in that not a single state that has become "shall issue" over the last twenty years has entirely removed arbitrary and unofficial authority to determine suitability in deciding who shall own and carry guns. Furthermore, in the wake of the 2008 Heller decision which explicitly recognized the Constitutional right of citizens to keep a gun in their residence for self-defense, there has not been a single successful effort to extend this Constitutional protection to carrying guns outside the home.

I make these points because the NRA and its self-appointed promoters like John Lott consistently refer to the large increase in CCW permits nationwide as some kind of "proof" that a great legal tidal wave of less-restrictive gun laws shows how increasingly pro-gun the American public has become. And while there is no doubt that applications and approvals for

CCW have risen significantly in the last decade, it is not clear whether this is because new shooters are entering the gun market and are more oriented towards concealed-carry than the previous generations, or because more talk is going around about the virtues of CCW, thus leading older gun owners to go beyond gun ownership and also make themselves legally able to carry a concealed gun. Either way, there's no question that John Lott's book and subsequent writing/commenting/blogging has been a significant factor in promoting the social utility of guns as keeping us safer from crime. So let's dig more deeply into what he has said.

As opposed to Gary Kleck, who based his argument about DGU specifically and only on data that his telephone survey group collected from interviews with random individuals who claimed to have carried out a DGU, Lott's data for arguing an inverse relationship between CCW and crime rates comes from a variety of sources, none of which, I should add, are explicitly described either in terms of what they contain or the time-period that they cover. The crime data, for example, comes from the Uniform Crime Reports from 1977 to 2005, but even Lott admits that the data is more complete for certain years and jurisdictions than others (although nowhere does he actually describe the parameters of any of his data-sets). He also has minimal data on the actual number of concealed-carry permits issued by the states in which CCW law was changed during the period covered in the book, forcing him to assume that criminal behavior was influenced not by actual encounters with armed citizens but rather some kind of awareness that a shift to non-discretionary (i.e. shall-issue) CCW would then result in more citizens walking around with guns. For reasons I will explain below, I find this premise of a connection between changes in the law and perceptions held by criminals about armed resistance to their activities to be not only unproven by Lott, but questioned neither by him or, for that matter, by his critics, of whom there have been many.

In fact, almost from the day the first edition of the book appeared, if not from an article on the same subject that he published in 1997, Lott has been the subject of a remarkable degree of negative scholarly attention, provoked to a certain extent by the immediate promotion of his ideas via a well-orchestrated campaign led by the pro-gun lobby, aka the NRA.[7] Shortly after the 1997 article was published, Senator Larry Craig (the one who couldn't keep himself out of public bathrooms, you may recall) introduced The Personal Safety and Community Protection Act, which was the first effort, followed over the years by many others, to grant state-to-state reciprocity for concealed-carry licenses, much as we all can drive across through the 50 states even though our driver's license is issued by our legal state of residence. To understand the role that Lott has played in the debate over the social utility of guns, it's worth quoting Craig's statement about his bill at length:

> The benefits of right-to-carry laws were verified by a landmark study released late last year. Following a comprehensive analysis of annual FBI crime statistics from all the Nation's counties, over 15 years, the authors concluded: [a]llowing citizens to carry concealed weapons deters violent crimes and it appears to produce no increase in accidental death or suicides. If those states who did not have concealed gun provisions had adopted them in 1992, approximately 1,800 murders and over 3,000 rapes would have been avoided yearly.[8]

Two years later, in 1999, Lott testified before the House Judiciary Committee at which time he attacked a Clinton gun control proposal as something that would actually cost lives, and he also appeared frequently at various state legislative hearings, covering concealed-carry laws in at least five states that were either considering a new CCW law or revising an existing one. In 2002, his work was cited when 18 state Attorneys General (who happened to be Republicans) wrote to then-Attorney General Ashcroft supporting the Administration's decision to consider the 2nd Amendment as protecting the individual right to own guns, an administrative action which played a not-unimportant role in advancing federal jurisprudence on 2nd Amendment cases that eventually led to the Heller decision in 2008.

I would not be underestimating Lott's value to the pro-gun community if I were to say that his book, along with his endless attempts to promote it on every conservative-leaning media outlet, played an important, if not the most important role in creating a climate of public opinion in which the social utility of guns was viewed increasingly in positive terms. It therefore should not have come as any surprise to Lott that criticisms of his work went far beyond what normally would have emerged from the public health scholarly community that, by and large, was developing a definition of firearm social utility that would result in less, rather than more access to guns. Concerns about the way in which he analyzed publicly-available data were compounded when he was unable to produce private survey information which he claimed showed that virtually everyone who used a gun defensively did so without actually pulling the trigger. Not only couldn't he produce the data from his own alleged national survey, he also couldn't remember the names of any of the individuals who helped him conduct the survey.[9] He made matters worse when he admitted that he invented an online persona named Mary Rosh who posted flattering tributes to his teaching abilities on various websites; his excuse that this was to protect himself from further attacks against his credibility only diminished his credibility even further.

I'm not going to spend any time discussing Lott's personal behavior or make any judgments about whether such activities discredit or impugn his published efforts as a whole. I will say it should come as no surprise that if a scholar produces research that is used to promote conservative public policies, particularly policies related in any manner to public health issues, he or she should be prepared to accept a higher and more critical degree of scrutiny from other scholars then would be the case if the work in question promoted liberal policy ends. Liberal thinking is pervasive in the social and health sciences, and anyone who believes that they can exert a conservative influence over discussions in these fields without provoking a larger share of attention than what might be otherwise warranted is, at best, naïve and at worst, cynically attempting to deflect honest criticism by pretending that all negative comments are driven only by bias rather than the search for truth.

I tend to think that Lott veers much more to the latter position than the former. To the extent that he is considered by conservative media to be a "go to" resource on issues about guns, it doesn't detract from his audience appeal that he is frequently and often caustically attacked from the Left. But again I'm not going to push myself in the direction of joining the argument either for or against the behavior of John Lott. My interest is in the manner in which he creates an argument for the social utility of guns, an argument that has remained the central component of pro-gun rhetoric to the present day. Because the ultimate point of his work is not just to show that as more Americans own and carry guns the crime rate goes down, but that the result of a generalized decrease in crime is a significant savings of what otherwise would be the cost of crime. So the social utility of firearm ownership is not justified by personal protection per se, but how increased personal protection saves society what otherwise would be the financial outlay caused by higher rates of crime.

Lott's study aggregated and then compared two basic trends: crime rates and issuance of CCW permits. But he didn't have any numbers for how many permits were issued, he just looked at violent crime rates before and after CCW permits were either approved for the first time in each state or were made non-discretionary so that, in theory, more gun owners could qualify for concealed-carry of their guns. What he claimed to have found in most of the states where CCW laws were introduced or revised between 1977 and 2005 (twenty-nine states) was an 8% decline in murders, a 5% decline in rapes and a 7% decline in aggravated assaults.[10] At the same time, while violent crimes against individuals went down, property crimes increased, a natural result, according to Lott, of criminals "choosing to commit less risky crimes that involve minimal contact with the victim."[11] If one then deducted the cost of violent crimes that were not committed and added back in the cost of additional property crimes, the resultant cost of crime over the period reviewed, according to Lott, showed a plus of $5.7 billion. Notice that Lott's argument for social utility was not based on self-protection per se, which was at the heart of Kleck's thesis, but the idea that CCW would result in a *change in criminal behavior*, thus benefitting society as a whole. To quote further from Senator Craig's statement that was made when he championed national concealed-carry:

> The primary author of the study, John R. Lott Jr. of the University of Chicago Law

School, has pointed out that the benefits of concealed-carry laws are not limited to those who carry the weapons but extend to their fellow citizens, as well. The drop in crime is not necessarily the result of using firearms in self-defense, but of criminals changing their behavior to avoid coming into direct contact with a person who might have a gun—which in a concealed-carry State could extend to a wide cross-section of the public.[12]

By framing his social utility argument in terms of the financial value of concealed-carry, Lott was not just arguing for CCW on the grounds of personal security, he was elevating the argument to a level of utility that would benefit society as a whole, including people who did not own guns or didn't want to carry them around even if they did own them. And from that time forward, gun advocates, the NRA in particular, would champion gun ownership as a civic responsibility and a patriotic response to the unquestioned need of society to protect itself from violence and crime.

Having done a good deal of research on the mechanics, legalities and personal practices surrounding CCW, the first thing that came to mind when I read Lott's book was his utter and complete failure to distinguish or even mention any distinction between the passage of a CCW law and the diffusion or spread of CCW permits within the jurisdiction covered by the law. Not only was he unable to gather anything more than a smattering of data on how many permits were issued after non-discretionary CCW laws were passed, he certainly couldn't calculate or even pretend to know the number of gun owners who, even if they received a CCW license, were now taking the trouble to walk around armed.

Kleck didn't have this problem when he did his research, because his research plan consciously avoided the issue of the origin or status of the guns allegedly used by respondents to thwart what otherwise might have been the commission of a crime. Of course this strategy helped get around the messy issue of having to validate the respondent's declaration that, in fact, a DGU had actually occurred; but it also allowed Kleck to posit a total DGU number in the millions regardless of how many active concealed-carry permits existed in the jurisdictions whose residents provided positive responses to his survey.

Since Lott had no way of knowing the practical effects of CCW laws in terms of who was actually walking around with a gun, he had no choice but to hypothesize that the net effect of a new or less-restrictive CCW law was the result not of encounters between criminals and newly-armed citizens, but was the result of a mental shift in criminal behavior, given the possibility that the criminal now had to consider the greater likelihood that the intended victim of his criminal attack would be armed. And what did Lott use to prove his theory that CCW made criminals change their behavior? He used his calculations which showed that while violent crimes against persons dropped by 5-7% for homicide, rape and aggravated assault, property crimes increased slightly in jurisdictions with new CCW laws, because criminals made a rational decision to shift their criminality away from face-to-face activities and hence, less risky crimes.[13]

In my mind this has got to be one of the dumbest and shoddiest theories about criminal behavior ever presented anywhere; namely, the idea that someone who might otherwise commit a homicide will consciously choose to substitute another type of crime because the homicide might be too risky to carry out. More than 4 out of 5 homicides involve perpetrators and victims who know each other (Lott's attempt to argue otherwise is pure nonsense tinged with the usual "gang membership" malarkey), it is a classical impulsive, unplanned act, and it usually emerges from a long-standing and continuous dispute either between street-corner denizens over who will control a particular piece of urban sidewalk, or between intimate partners over who will do whatever angry intimate partners do. That such behavior could be methodically and rationally channeled into a conscious crime-substitution strategy is either the result of scholarly dementia or reflects the fact that Lott knew that his intended audience wouldn't really care what he said anyway, as long as he made them feel justified to carry a gun.

Yet critical response to this half-cocked notion, indeed the response to the entirety of Lott's work, was to avoid discussing this substitution theory and instead focus on the methodological shortcomings of his statistical analysis, which nevertheless came to the same negative conclusion about the shift from violent to property crimes in the wake of new CCW laws. But in the case of scholars who found his argument insufficient from a methodological point of view, it turns out that when several critics attempted to replicate his results by using his data in ways they considered to be more theoretically valid, not only did property crime increase after laws were changed, but violent crimes increased as well.[14] These results had to do with applying different and more realistic criteria for the inclusion or exclusion of certain jurisdictions, as well as slightly shifting the time-span covered by the study relative to the dates at which CCW laws were changed.

Readers will please forgive me for presenting both the arguments made by Lott as well as his critics in less than technical terms. If anyone wants to wade through hundreds of pages of charts, graphs and statistical jargon, the endnotes to this chapter supply all the sources you need. You can assume, however, that my avoidance of technical and detailed explanations in no way alters the basic findings both of Lott as well as the scholars who closely examined his work. The bottom line that differentiated the two positions was simply that Lott found an overwhelming concordance between the ability of many jurisdictions to issue CCW and a drop in certain categories of violent crime, while the other side found that after CCW was instituted, a majority of jurisdictions experienced an increase in both violent and property crimes. These findings also resulted in a re-examination of Lott's argument about the financially beneficial impact of CCW, with the $5.6 billion in savings going away and leaving a deficit of $1 billion resulting from the passage of concealed-carry laws.[15]

In the wake of the controversy that erupted after Lott published his book, the author of *More Guns, Less Crime* often charged critics with, among other things, falsely claiming that CCW increased crime rates because concealed-carry license holders were committing this additional crime. There certainly were objections voiced against CCW on that basis whenever a public debate on a CCW law broke out. Bu the scholars who challenged Lott's findings on the basis of faulty methodology or slipshod statistical analysis were never part of any such group. In fact, to the contrary, I found the scholarly critiques of Lott's research to be not only restrained but somewhat balanced in their reactions to his work. For example, Ayres and Donohue in a 2003 review of Lott's book (that ran almost as many pages as the book itself) said the following: "At the end of the day, then, it is still possible that shall-issue laws have no effect—positive or negative—on crime."[16] In other words, what Lott allegedly proved and what these scholars then disproved may cancel one another out. We will return to this specific issue in Chapter 6 when we review how that august body—the National Academy of Sciences—dealt with all the scholarly arguments, pro and con, covering the social utility of guns.

My issue with Lott, however, is not based on whether his statistical package is more robust than the statistical analyses developed by his critics. Nor am I really concerned with the shortcomings and gaps in his data based either on the choice of jurisdictions (states versus counties) or the span of years. Rather, it has to do with the question of intent. Because I simply cannot dismiss the coincidence that the research for this book was conducted at exactly the same time that the NRA and the gun lobby were beginning to use CCW as their strongest argument for the positive social utility of guns. Which meant that Kleck's "discovery" of millions of unreported DGUs was not enough, because this simply justified gun ownership for the individual who wanted to own a gun. Lott, on the other hand, was saying that guns protected *everyone* against crime. And not a single scholar who took Lott to task for his statistical insufficiencies or data gaps bothered to point this out. To the contrary, they all accepted his harebrained substitution theory of criminal behavior as if this could serve as a meaningful explanation for the contrast between rates of violent versus property crimes. By framing their reactions to Lott's work within the polite parameters of this statistical analysis versus that statistical analysis, scholars who should have been raising the issue of Lott's true intentions let the whole question slide quietly by.

Notwithstanding my comments above about the liberal tilt of social science and public health research, I find that members of the scholarly guild who question the positive social utility arguments made by

Kleck and Lott tend to frame their questions in a very polite way. Even scholars who, in private, agree with my thoughts that Kleck and Lott at best are mediocre researchers, and at worst charlatans and self-promoters, tend in public to give them the benefit of the doubt. By which I mean that in subjecting their work to reasoned, serious analysis, they are creating the notion that this work deserves scholarly attention at all.

I am not sure of the reasons for this public show of deference to writings which, objectively, deserve to be considered as nothing other than trash. Part of it no doubt reflects the standard, academically-approved behavior that often uses a deft *politesse* style to frame disagreements of any sort. Part of it is also the necessity to create, as it were, a "legitimate" scholarly opponent, because how otherwise could scholars who argue for gun control justify the importance and relevance of what they are attempting to prove? And perhaps there is even a slight tinge of concern on the part of academically-based researchers that maintaining an elevated rhetoric and style is what they presume their audiences expect will come from them.

Like the battle between advocacy groups, here again when it comes to motives and strategies the gun control folks simply don't understand. The NRA and the gun lobby don't promote gun research which advances their point of view because they have any interest in research. Their interest, like that of any industry trade group, is to get their point of view out to the public so that any public policy relevant to their products impacts them as positively as possible. And since public policies, by definition, are created to prevent things from happening that otherwise happen without policies, research like the stuff done by Kleck and Lott is designed to forestall any public gun policy at all. The whole approach of the NRA, as I pointed out with reference to Kleck's affidavit before the Federal District Court in Heller II, is to advance the notion that gun laws should only be enacted to deal with how and when "bad guys" use guns. And if you can produce "evidence" which purports to prove that gun ownership has a positive social utility, then this only gives more weight to the argument that guns in the hands of average, law-abiding citizens don't need to be the subject of any public policy at all.

I am neither surprised nor dismayed by this approach to research on the part of the NRA; but I am somewhat surprised and dismayed that public health researchers and other academics would assume that when they look at pro-gun publications by people like Kleck and Lott, that they are looking at material which has been prepared to be taken seriously in the public policy debate. On the other hand, if there wasn't a public debate then it is doubtful that we would have much interest in research from the other side, and just as Brady would have to invent the NRA if it didn't exist, so at the very least Kleck and Lott provide convenient targets (no pun intended) for much of the research produced by experts who want public policy to result in more control over guns. It is to the good and bad news about such research that we now turn.

CHAPTER 4

ENTER PUBLIC HEALTH—MORE GUNS EQUALS MORE GUN VIOLENCE

The last two chapters covered how scholars representing the pro-gun community have constructed an argument for the positive social utility of guns. Now I am going to look at the arguments for a negative social utility of guns as developed by the gun-control community. But before I look at their two most important arguments, I need to spend a bit of time talking about something on which both sides appear to agree, namely, the number of guns. The overwhelming number of firearms in civilian hands is used by both sides to justify their arguments about the positive or negative social utility of firearms; the pro-gun side says that since guns make us safer, the more guns the better; the anti-gun side says that since guns make us less safe, the more guns there are, the less safe we become. So both sides have an interest in promoting the highest figure of civilian-owned guns that they can. Which still leaves the open question:

How many of the damn things are really floating around?

The usual number given for American civilian ownership of small arms is 300 million. This figure is accepted by the United Nations and everyone else. Where does it come from? Good question. Since guns are not registered except at the initial point of sale, and this practice, known as the NICS background check, only started in 1998 and covered each transaction regardless of how many guns were purchased at the time the transaction took place, the only numbers we have are based on aggregate reports from manufacturers and importers as to how many guns they put into the market each year.[1] But we have no idea what percentage of those products, particularly over time, are still either usable or in someone's active possession and therefore should be counted as part of the civilian arsenal.

But the more compelling problem has to do with the fact that if we are trying to figure out how many guns are floating around that might be used to commit acts of intentional gun violence (homicides, robberies, assaults and suicides), the overall number of extant civilian guns is a somewhat meaningless figure because 80-90% of all gun violence takes place with handguns. And while the percentage of handguns manufactured and imported each year keeps climbing relative to the number of overall guns, throwing around a number like 300 million when we are arguing about what to do about gun violence is to throw around a number without any real significance at all.

The problem is that both sides in the gun argument prefer to use the global number of 300 million or more because it fits the agendas of both groups: the gun lobby loves the idea that there are as many guns as possible out there because this justifies their argument that guns are a normal product that everyone should own. The anti-gun folks also love to throw around the 300 million number because it is a much more alarming statistic if you are trying to make the argument that more guns equals more violence and more violent crime.

The problem with the argument about the number of guns is that it really doesn't have much to do with whether guns are used to prevent or commit crime and violence because the majority of the guns that are owned by Americans would never be involved in anything having to do with the social utility of the product. This is because if we define gun violence in its criminal form—homicide, assault, robbery—most of the guns used in this way are handguns which comprise less than half the guns under private ownership at the present time; in fact, probably a good deal less than half. Kleck, for example, tells us that less than 20% of the privately-owned guns in the mid-60's were handguns, a percentage which began to climb as we move in to the 1970's, but even in the 1980's, when gun sales started to escalate to record levels, long gun sales still matched handguns in terms of domestic manufacture, and remained the majority of small arms imported from overseas.[2]

What all of this adds up to is that any argument, pro or con, about the social utility of guns that is based on the image of U.S. gun ownership as being almost equal to, or perhaps larger than one gun for every resident, has absolutely nothing to do with the issue of social utility of small arms. This is not only true in the aggregate, but just as true when broken down to specific localities. For example, pro-gun advocates love to cite per capita gun ownership numbers to "prove" that the anti-gun forces have no idea what they are talking about when they claim that more guns equals more violence and crime. They cite as an example of this situation the gun ownership levels in Western states like the Dakotas, Montana and so forth, where the number of guns owned by state residents are far beyond the number of residents, yet gun crimes, particularly homicides, are some of the lowest of all the states.[3] What this argument ignores, however, is that gun ownership in Western states tilts towards long guns which are rarely used in criminal events. Conversely, these same pro-gun advocates cite violent crime rates in gun-free cities like Washington, D.C., where the number of legally-owned guns falls so far short of the number of city residents that, on a per capita basis, the District of Columbia contains virtually no guns at all. But how difficult is it to carry a small, concealed handgun from one jurisdiction to another? My state, Massachusetts, does not allow the purchase of fireworks. Guess what kind of a store is located closest to the state line when you cross over into New Hampshire?

In addition to not knowing how many handguns are owned by U.S. residents, the bigger problem is trying to figure out how many of those handguns are in the hands of people who aren't supposed to be able to get their hands on a gun. If we had some idea of the actual ratio of legal to illegal possession of handguns we could at least formulate some strategy for controlling or eradicating the guns that are used to commit crimes. Absent such a number, people who advocate more controls over guns as a way of keeping them out of the "wrong" hands have no choice but to advocate greater control over all guns, whether this impinges unfairly on legal gun owners or not.

How many guns are used each year in the commission of crimes? According to the FBI, there were 8,000 gun homicides, 122,000 gun robberies and 143,000 gun assaults in 2012.[4] If every one of these crimes involved the use of a different gun, roughly 270,000 guns were used to commit violent crime. Now let's assume that 80 percent of these guns were handguns, although this is by far a low estimate. But since this is the official percentage of handgun crimes, so says the FBI, for the moment we'll stay with it. Now according to the DOJ, 1.4 million guns were stolen between 2005 and 2010, or an average of approximately 230,000 per year.[5] This is an estimate based on responses to the NCVS survey which asked respondents to tell what kinds of items were taken from them in crimes. It is probably a pretty good number. Which means that even if not a single gun got into the wrong hands by dint of being purchased by someone who then either consciously or unconsciously transferred the gun to a "wrong hands" kind of guy, the volume of stolen and lost guns in and of itself is probably large enough to fill the needs of gun-using criminals each year.

But again this data begs the issue of whether the guns that are lost or stolen are "crime" guns, so to speak, aka handguns, and I suspect this is not the case. If anything, guns are often reported stolen so that insurance can be collected, and many more long guns are insured under general homeowner policies than hand guns. This is because long guns, particularly those that have been in a family's possession for several generations, are considered to be heirlooms and prized family possessions; handguns rarely attain such a coveted status. The point is that if someone breaks into a house and steals a long gun, there's a pretty good chance it will be reported to the police but a pretty small chance that it will ever be used in a crime. When it comes to the theft or loss of a handgun, the ratio probably works in exactly the other way. Many less reported, many more ending up in the "wrong hands."

What about the issue of "rogue" dealers who sell many guns that are either picked up in crimes or sell guns in which the "time to crime" is very brief? This issue may consist of the biggest pile of unmitigated horseshit to come out of the entire argument about guns. So I am going to spend a few paragraphs going into this issue in detail. First of all we have the so-called gun "trafficking" problem which was brought into public view with great fanfare when Mike Bloomberg first began talking about all those crime guns that were being shipped to New York. Bloomberg's group, Mayors Against Illegal Guns, issued a report which then turned into an interactive web site that allows the viewer to click on any state and learn whether the state in question is a "net importer" or "net exporter" of guns.[6] In 2009, New York was a net gun importer to the tune of 3,607 crime guns coming in and 517 crime guns going out.

Bloomberg earlier made real headlines when his group put undercover videos online which showed several dealers conducting "straw sales" of their guns to Bloomberg employees, activities which were then followed by law suits against these and other dealers filed by New York City for aiding and/or abetting illegal sales of guns which ended up being used in New York crimes. These suits didn't go anywhere but they created the public impression that gun "trafficking" was a major source of guns that were eventually used in crimes. Several months after Sandy Hook, a major gun trafficking bill was introduced in the Senate which took the notion of an individual "straw sale," (one person buying a gun for someone else who is prohibited from buying a gun) and applied it to the purchase of multiple guns with a maximum sentence of *fifteen years*. Wow! Guess where the bill ended up?

The idea that lots of crime guns are flooding the streets because a few gun dealers were using their gun shops as fronts for major gun trafficking operations had been given additional credence beyond

Bloomberg's activities by a series of stories in the Washington Post, "The Hidden Life of Guns," which found that from 1998 through 2009, there were 40 gun dealers in Virginia who between them sold 2,371 guns that were later picked up in crimes.[7] That's more than two hundred crime guns a year or an average of five crime guns per dealer. That's a lot of guns, right? Let me break it to you gently. Over this same time-frame, these dealers sold over *800,000* guns. Not eight thousand, not eighty thousand, but eight *hundred thousand* guns. In other words, two-tenths of one percent of the guns they sold ended up being picked up by various police departments as illegal guns. And of those two-tenths of one percent of guns that these bad dealers sold, almost half were picked up in what is known as "weapons violations," a grab-bag term that can mean anything from a gun being shot off accidentally but illegally to a gun in the home of someone convicted of a crime that has nothing to do with using a gun but still means the person can't own a gun, to all kinds of other legal issues which don't necessarily mean that the person from whom the gun was confiscated was ever going to use it in a criminal or violent way. Know how many of these crime guns were actually used in violent crimes? A grand total of 404 guns out of the 2,371 picked up by the cops. Or to put it another way, of the 800,000 guns that these rogue dealers sold, one-half of one one-thousandths of them (0.0005) were used in violent crimes.

But let's not blame the *Washington Post* for trying to milk a good story out of a few jumbled facts. After all, it's a newspaper, right? They have to come up with some kind of story, don't they? If we are going to understand the true scope of gun trafficking, let's go to the source, the organization responsible for tracing guns, aka the ATF, which publishes a very comprehensive report (found in the *Statistics* section of the ATF website) on yearly gun traces covering every state since 2006.[8] And here are the national trace numbers for various types of traces in 2013:

Reason for Trace	**No. Traces**	**% all Traces**
Assault	11,650	4.7%
Burglary	9,563	3.9%
Dangerous Drugs	27,587	11.2%
Firearm Under Investigation	32,134	13.1%
Found Firearm	21,619	8.8%
Homicide	6,854	2.8%
Possession of Weapon	61,439	25.0%
Robbery	4,690	1.9%
Weapons Offense	18,001	7.3%
TOTAL ALL TRACES	245,749	

Notice that 22% of all traces involved guns that were "under investigation" or "found." Those are really serious crimes. Nearly one-third of the traces were either for weapons illegally possessed or some kind of "offense" with a weapon. Where I live you can have a gun confiscated if you discharge it within 200 feet of a road. That's an offense. Don't get me wrong. I'm not trying to make light of the fact that guns can be used to do terrible damage or help commit terrible crimes. I'm only trying to bring a little perspective into the notion that 20% of all traced guns in the United States were traced in less than three years after they were purchased; this doesn't mean that all these guns were bought so they could immediately or at any time be put into the "wrong" hands. But if you listen to some of the experts on guns and crime, you would think that every time a gun is traced that was just sold over the counter, it was sold to someone or by someone who was up to no good.

What I love is the nearly 9% of all traces that were for "found firearms." Which means, if I know how to read English, that someone picked up a gun from a trash can, or a locker, or the sidewalk, or somewhere else and turned it into the cops. In New York, it was 13% of all traces, in Wyoming it was 17%. I would really like to know how many of the "found" weapons were either returned to their rightful owner or represented guns that the old man had in his basement and after he was packed off to the nursing home and the kids ransacked the place, nobody wanted any of his old junk, a category that included his guns. I have a good friend who just celebrated his 70th birthday and he was a gun salesman for close to 50 years. He has four children, all now grown and married, and all of them were raised in a comfortable home thanks to their father who spent his working life selling guns. Over the years my friend put together a pretty nice gun collection and recently asked his children if they wanted to take any of the weapons as a memory of their father, to which he was told a very definitive "no." Luckily, he mentioned this episode to me and I was able to purchase two of his guns. But if he were to outlive his wife and then one day moved on to his great reward, his kids would clean the house out and the guns would be dumped or just left behind. Or sold for pennies. Or just thrown out. And if they are thrown out the trash collector will find them in the bottom of some barrel out at the curb and they will eventually wind up being listed by the ATF as "found guns."

The police chief in my town, like myself, is a gun nut. And every couple of months or so our nuttiness gets tested when he gets a phone call from some family member who just put Pop or Mom in the nursing home and are in the process of cleaning out the old place and open a closet or a cedar cabinet and there sits the old man's guns. This is not unusual in my town because many of the older residents worked for Smith & Wesson or Savage Arms or Harrington & Richardson, three gun factories that are easy commuting distance with steady work and a decent end-of-week check. In fact, the long-time manager of Smith & Wesson, Carl Hellstrom, used to come out to the Polish parish in my town and recruit guys to come to work the following day because Smith & Wesson always paid on a piece-work basis and Hellstrom knew that the Polacks in my town would sit in the fitting room or the assembly room until Hell froze over turning out those perfectly-chamfered cylinders and immaculately-polished slides because they were getting a half-buck for every piece they turned out.

So the Chief gets the call to come over and pick up the guns because none of the surviving kids know what to do with the damn things, and he always stops by and takes me along in case the kids want to make a cash deal for the old clunkers right then and there. I can tell you that on our way to the house we always fantasize that we'll find a beautiful Colt Single Action Army revolver like the kind that Gary Cooper carried in *High Noon,* or maybe there will be one of those Winchester repeating rifles with the extra-wide lever that John Wayne stuck under his saddle in *Red River,* but it's never to be. What we find every time is junk.

That's right, just junk. So I offer the kids a ten or a twenty and they're happy to get rid of the crap without having to go through this legal nonsense or that.

But know what the Chief has to do before he can give the guns to me? He has to make sure they weren't stolen by sending a trace request to the ATF. That's right. The law in my state requires that no police department can confiscate or otherwise hold a gun unless it is first checked against the "missing/stolen" list compiled by the ATF. And do you think for one second that any of these guns was actually reported stolen or missing over the previous forty years? For that matter, do you believe that the ATF could ever figure out when or where those guns were sold for the first time? One of the very nice ladies who runs the missing/stolen list told me (I'll not give her name for obvious reasons) that of the trace requests that she receives from police departments every day, more than one-third were missing information—name of manufacturer, serial number—which would allow her to conduct a trace at all. Know when serial numbers were required on all newly-manufactured guns? The Gun Control Act of 1968. Sears Roebuck sold a very nice shotgun endorsed by Ted Williams back in the 1950's, ditto a gun sold by J.C. Higgins. Some had serial numbers, some not. Want to use the ATF trace list to figure out how guns get into the "wrong hands?" You go right ahead. Go figure.

Here's the point of the last few pages. We have no idea how many guns are really floating around and we certainly don't know about when and why guns get into the "wrong" hands. So the notion that there must be some connection between all those guns out there and the level of gun violence, while intuitively probably correct, is far from being proven by anything other than intuition and some kind of blind assumption that it must be true because nobody has shown it to be false. We know that street guns start getting into the hands of kids in their early teenage years, and while some estimates put at 5% the number of kids who bring guns into school, the pattern is noticed in many school districts by the 6th or 7th grade.[9] The major study on kids acquiring guns was published by Daniel Webster and colleagues in 2002, and he found that the younger kids generally got their hands on guns because it was the "cool" thing to do, but the desire to acquire or possess a gun became more job-related (i.e., committing crimes or protecting oneself from a competitive criminal) as teens grew into adults.[10]

One of the interesting things that Philip Cook learned when he studied the illegal gun market was that, other than a complete absence of administrative controls such as background checks and the like, the gun market that existed outside the law operated similar to the lawful market; i.e., older purchasers preferred more expensive guns and prices paid for street-corner guns weren't that different from what the same guns cost if purchased in a normal way.[11] It also seems to be the case that street guns are often owned or possessed in common; i.e., they move around from person to person based on need for a specific use rather than just being carried around the like a phone in the pocket. One of the major reasons for this quaint communalism of gun ownership amongst the criminal population is the knowledge that being caught with a gun, particularly one that could be linked to a crime, would result in a much lengthier jail sentence, as opposed to being convicted of a serious crime for which in many cases absent a gun would result in little or no jail time at all.

Notwithstanding all of the above, including the fact that the demand for guns by people who just can't walk into a gun shop and buy a gun could probably be met simply through theft and loss without the additional enhancements to the illegal arsenal by professional gun traffickers (if, indeed there are such people), the truth is that we simply do not know in any tangible form how guns move from legal to illegal hands. And because we don't know how this occurs, it seems to me rather pointless to keep talking about the fact that the existence of 300 million guns is the *prima facie* reason why we have so much gun violence and gun crime. After all, the public argument about guns isn't about guns per se. It's about whether guns make us a more or less safe society. And as long as we don't know how guns end up being used to make us less safe (which then provokes more people to carry guns to make us more safe), the only thing we can do to resolve the problem is get rid of the guns. Even the most ardent gun controllers among us at least tacitly adhere to the notion that the 2nd Amendment means that guns are here to stay. They may not really believe it in their heart of hearts, but they say it. And because they say it, that have to advance public policies that take such statements into account.

This being the case, I think that using the existence of 300 million or more guns as the reason why we have a gun violence "problem" is to construct a blind alley for two reasons: (1) We are not going to get rid of all the guns; (2) Given #1, how do we go about controlling some guns so as to reduce the effect (violence) of the existence of all guns? The problem with the public health approach to gun violence, which is what stands behind virtually all the research done on the negative social utility of guns, is that it presumes that guns are a universal phenomenon whose effects can be measured in the same way as we measure, for example, the results of using seat belts. Note that when I talk about "measurement" I am not talking about measuring the amount of gun violence that we currently experience; rather, I speak of the measurement of gun violence levels if we had more controls over how many or what kinds of guns were out there. Nevertheless, the assumption that our elevated levels of violence are due to the existence of all those guns is the fundamental axiom upon which all public health research on gun violence rests.

Let's examine the public health arguments in detail, or what I would call the negative social utility of guns. The global argument that more guns make us less safe has been the handiwork in particular of David Hemenway and his research associates of the Injury Prevention Control Center at the Harvard School of Public Health. In the interests of full disclosure I should point out that David and his colleagues are my academic friends and I value their commitment and dedication to advancing public health. And if anyone wants to say that my comparison of the value of their work to the work of Kleck and Lott is somehow tainted because of this personal and professional connection, go right ahead and say it.

The notion of causality between the number of guns and the high rate of gun violence is most clearly and recently discussed in an article co-authored by Hemenway that appeared in 2011 in The *Journal of Trauma,* that was based on data initially made available in 2003.[12] In this article, which followed from Hemenway's earlier book, *Private Guns, Public Health*, he compared homicide, suicide and injury rates of 23 advanced countries, known as the Organization for Economic Co-Operation and Development countries (OECD), that supplied relevant mortality and morbidity data to the WHO. It should be noted, incidentally, that these are more or less the same countries whose health care is compared to our health care each year, comparisons which invariably show that our health care system lags far behind other OECD countries in terms of quality of care. It's not really true, but (a brief self-advertisement follows) that book will have to wait until I finish writing these books on guns.

When it comes to comparing the number of suicides, homicides and unintentional mortalities with guns, however, the US isn't behind as in the case of health care, but rather is very far out front of the rest of the OECD. In 2003 the US homicide rate was nearly seven times higher than the rates in other OECD countries, with a gun homicide rate that was 19.5 times higher. The US gun suicide rate was almost 6 times higher than other countries and the gun mortality rate was more than 5 times higher. Interestingly, while the US was far ahead of all OECD countries in the use of guns for suicides, homicides and unintentional gun deaths, the prevalence of firearms did not make us a more violent society per se. Hemenway is careful to note that our overall violent crime rate was equal or lower than crime rates in other OECD countries, and the use of guns for suicide did not drive our overall suicide rate higher than suicide rates elsewhere. Do such findings therefore show either a negative social utility for guns or counteract the Kleck-Lott argument about the positive social utility of guns? Not really.

For the latter argument one needs to turn to another article published by Hemenway in 2011 in which he explicitly compares the positive versus negative social utilities of firearm ownership.[13] The good news about this article is that it not only draws on Hemenway's own research but is rather a summary of the major work conducted by public health researchers over the previous twenty years; hence, it should be read as a basic "state of the argument" analysis of public health research on guns.

Hemenway begins this article by setting the basic parameters of the discussion, namely, the existence of so many guns: "Americans have more private guns per capita, and particularly more handguns, than citizens of other developed countries." He can't give any reliable figures on the ratio of handguns to long guns, because as I have said throughout this book and in my other books, there aren't any such numbers beyond what the ATF says were the number of guns, by category, manufactured and imported each year. But what he does note, and this is an awareness that is too-often lacking in the work of people who advocate the negative social utility of guns, is that American gun ownership is skewed by geography, culture and political attitudes; the fact that we have almost as many guns per capita as we have people living in the US does not mean that every one of them owns a gun.

And this is a very important and often overlooked point, namely, the geography of firearm ownership. Because the United States is often best understood if we think of the country in terms of regions, and woe betide the public policy planner, particularly regarding gun policy, who doesn't take our very strong regionalism into account. For example, I have noted previously that gun ownership is much more pronounced in the South, the rural

Midwest and the mountain states of the West, with per capita ownership easily exceeding one gun for every person living in these regions. But per capita gun ownership in the Northeast, for example, is a fraction of the Western or Southern number, so what might work policy-wise in that part of the country won't fly at all in regions where guns are more prevalent. Hemenway is one of the public health researchers who is clearly sensitive to this problem; many of this colleagues are not.

Before I get into the details of his article, it should be noted that the title alone—risks and benefits—sets out what I believe is the correct context in which measurements of the positive-negative social utility of guns should be made. Hemenway, it seems to me, is the only researcher on either side of the issue who approaches the problem from a truly cost-benefit point of view which recognizes that what may be a positive social utility to one person could as well be a negative social utility to someone else. This is entirely different from other advocates and researchers on both sides who argue either for or against gun access without regard for whether both positions have a degree of intrinsic validity simply because they have decided to be for or against guns. For this reason I consider Hemenway's work to be the definitive statement about the social utility of guns. But "definitive" and "correct" aren't necessarily the same thing.

Hemenway begins his review by focusing on the risks of gun ownership, which he defines as accidents, suicides, homicides and intimidation. Surprisingly, he does not examine the issue of other violent crimes, like armed robbery or aggravated assaults, even though he later attempts to measure the benefits of gun ownership as including protection against such crimes. But for the moment let's stick with what he does discuss, beginning with unintentional injuries, both fatal and non-fatal. Research points to the fact that, according to Hemenway, for every unintentional death from guns each year, there are probably 10 self-inflicted injuries serious enough to require emergency room treatment. The latter number, I suspect, is far below the actual number of unintentional injuries that occur, because many accidents that are not considered life-threatening are probably treated by local physicians or health stations, particularly in rural areas where there are lots of guns. But for the moment let's stick with the official numbers generated through hospitalizations. In sum, an average of 7,500 people seriously hurt themselves or others with guns each year. The data also suggests that virtually all such accidents occur within the family and the home; often due to carelessness in cleaning or just handling the weapon, as in "didn't know it was loaded." They never know it was loaded.

As one would suspect, gun accidents occur more frequently in places where there are more guns. Hemenway compares accidental gun deaths to populations in states with high gun ownership (Western and Southern) versus states with low gun ownership (Northeast) and finds that residents of gun-rich states were 6 times more likely to die from gun wounds than residents in gun-poor states. For the country as a whole, the most vulnerable group are children under the age of 14, whose rate of accidental death from guns is 11 times higher than children of similar age in other OECD countries.

These numbers lead Hemenway to conclude that "the evidence indicates that a gun in the home is a risk factor for serious accidental injury." But how much of a risk is a risk? Accidental drownings, the majority of which occur in backyard pools, claimed 574 Americans ages 15-24 in 2004, the same year that accidental shootings killed 172 Americans in the same age group.[14] Of course, probably more people go swimming each year than own guns, but for the average American family, according to Professor Steven Levitt, the odds of a child being drowned in a backyard pool are 100 times higher than the same child being killed with a gun.[15]

The comparison of drownings to gun accidents is a favorite ploy of the gun lobby whenever they need to prove the positive social utility of guns. But the facts bear them out, not just in terms of numbers of accidents each year but also when one examines the overall trend. Because notwithstanding Hemenway's statement that unintentional gun mortalities were more than 680 per year between 2003 and 2007, this number represents a major decrease in accidental gun deaths when compared to a generation before. In 2004, there were 172 accidental shooting deaths for the age group 15-24 (this age group being the most vulnerable to gun deaths, both intentional and unintentional), but in 1993 this age group saw 595 deaths from unintentional shootings, a trend that can be found in every age group over the same period. And while drowning deaths in this age group declined by one-third from 1998 to 2008 (821 down to 569), accidental shooting deaths for ages 15-24 during the same period dropped fifty percent (260 to 132).[16] More to the point, over the last twenty years virtually every state passed laws requiring that backyard pools be fenced, particularly if the residence contains children, while the degree to which more than a handful of states have passed laws regulating gun safety range from negligible to nil. I'll hold off further discussion on this question of shooting trends until the concluding pages of the chapter, so let's turn to the issue of suicide, which Hemenway identifies as the second major risk of gun ownership.

I twice sold guns to customers in my shop who then used them to commit suicide. The first was an elderly man, I think he was past eighty, who came into the shop and purchased a used shotgun. He didn't exhibit any visible signs of distress and, in fact, he purchased the gun some months before he used it to end his life. I was later told by the cops that he lived alone and was perhaps in the throes of a terminal illness although nobody knew for sure. These end-of-life decisions by elderly people usually living alone, often in pain, are not uncommon and, as far as I am concerned, in many cases access to a gun makes it less difficult for someone to end their life in a simple and straightforward manner. Suicides of persons 85 years or older is the second most frequent age group, and I suspect that many of these individuals would not benefit to any great degree from intervention that would prevent them from carrying out the suicide attempt. This age group also uses guns to commit suicide to a greater degree than any other age group; a gun is the method in more than 80% of these suicides whereas guns are used overall in 50% of all suicides that occur each year.[17] While the suicide rate has risen slightly over the last few years, it is much more stable trend-wise than rates of unintentional injuries and homicides, both of which have declined substantially over the last several decades. The percentage of gun suicides overall has also been fairly stable.

The second customer in my gun shop who used his gun to kill himself was a 40-ish corrections officer who was married with children and, according to his wife, had been seeing a therapist, but neither the therapist nor she understood the extent of his depression. The way this situation was described to me by his widow illustrated the other side of gun suicide from the case of the old man mentioned above, namely, the ability of the victim to have access to a gun may have been a more precipitating factor than the depression which caused the suicide attempt in the first place. This is because most suicides, particularly in the most common age-group of 45–64 are immediate, impulsive events, often exacerbated by alcohol, usually stemming from an immediate problem which appears too big for the potential suicide victim to handle and, if stopped through often accidental intervention, end up never occurring again. As Hemenway notes, for most people "the risk period is transient. Reducing the availability of commonly used and lethal instruments during this period can prevent suicide."[18]

But Hemenway's argument assumes that if guns were removed, that the suicidal individual wouldn't find a substitute method to carry out a life-ending event? Can removing guns prevent suicide? Despite the existence of many studies which correlate gun ownership with what Hemenway calls "substantially and significantly" higher rates of suicide, it is not clear that any of these studies could adequately measure suicide rates in those homes if one were to create some kind of "substitution" effect; namely, taking the guns away from the suicide-prone population and then figuring out whether this would reduce the rate of suicide or just result in those individuals finding some other way to take their lives. I say this because, as opposed to unintentional injury and homicide, where the US rates are far higher than those found in other OECD countries (none of which have anywhere near the number of guns owned by the civilian population), the US suicide rate is not higher than suicide rates throughout the OECD. The US, for example, had an overall suicide rate in 2001 of 12 per 100,000; the rate in Britain was 11.8.[19] Meanwhile, the gun homicide rate in the US is twenty times higher than in the UK. Which means that while the relative lack of guns in England, particularly handguns, results in much less homicide, suicidal individuals in England are not deterred by the inability to get things over easily and quickly with access to a gun. Even Australia, which has a per capita rate of gun ownership roughly one-sixth the U.S. rate, has a suicide rate that is only 15% lower than the suicide rate in the US. It is therefore rather tenuous to conclude that, *ipso facto,* the existence of a civilian gun arsenal of more than 300 million weapons results in suicide as a clear risk.

On the other hand, when we look at whether guns are a risk factor in the issue of homicide, the evidence is overwhelming and compelling. Although the United States is not necessarily a more violent country than other OECD countries, in this case violence meaning all violent crime, our violence is much more lethal because of the existence of guns. And this is particularly true, according to the studies cited by Hemenway, when we look at certain subgroups within the overall population, in particular teenagers and young adults between 15 and 24 whose gun homicide rate is more than 40 times higher than the rate for this age group in other OECD countries. In addition to the linkage between guns and overall homicide rates, research cited by Hemenway also shows that homes containing guns have a much higher incidence of homicide than gun-free homes, even though most gun homicides occur in the street. When they do take place in a residence, women are a disproportionate number of the victims and virtually all residential homicides involve perpetrators and victims who knew each other prior to the assault.

While Hemenway presents persuasive data on the degree to which gun homicides are so much more prevalent in the US than in other Western countries whose private firearm arsenals are much smaller, he is careful not to assume a direct, causal linkage between access to guns and gun violence per se. He notes that studies which show increased homicide levels in homes with guns don't necessarily differentiate between the different types of individuals who live in homes with guns as opposed to gun-free homes, nor was it known whether the homicides were committed with guns from that particular home or from elsewhere. The fact that homes with guns were more apt to be places where gun homicides took place didn't necessarily mean that a gun used in a homicide couldn't have been brought into that home from somewhere else, thus reducing the correlation between gun homicides and the presence of a gun in those homes.

What I find interesting about Hemenway's discussion of gun homicide is that despite the disparity between rates of gun homicide in the US versus other advanced countries, I am not sure that this article makes a very strong case for the negative social utility of guns. And this is largely because of some issues that are not discussed in this article, although they have been mentioned by researchers elsewhere, but nevertheless would appear to be both relevant and necessary to examine in any attempt to judge the social utility of guns from a positive or negative perspective. The first issue has to do with race. Hemenway correctly points out that gun violence disproportionately impacts teens and young men between the ages of 15 and 24. Incidentally, this also happens to be the age cohort that figures most prominently in violent crime of all types. But alongside this age imbalance there is also a racial imbalance in American gun homicide, namely, the fact that more than two-thirds of all victims and perpetrators of gun homicide are African-American and Hispanic young men living in inner-city ghettos.

It simply cannot be ignored that two racial groups which together comprise less than 40% of the overall population furnish upwards of 70% of the population that commits or is the victim of gun homicides. And the reason that it cannot be ignored is that if we deduct these two groups from the total number of gun homicides, the overall homicide rate, while not coming down to levels recorded in other OECD countries, drops down substantially from the current rate and makes it less tenable to argue that our homicide rate is driven by gun homicides. For example, our current gun homicide rate is 3.6 per 100,000, France is .22, Germany is .20. But pull African-American and Hispanic numbers out of the overall count and our national homicide rate drops to 1.3; still higher than the OECD average of less than 1 per 100,000, but nowhere near the disparity that currently exists when we compare all of our gun homicides to numbers in other countries.

Using a national rate for comparison with other countries not only masks the degree to which our gun homicide rate is racially-based, but also hides severe disparities between different regions of the United States. So, while states like Louisiana and Missouri have gun homicide rates that are respectively twice and seventy percent higher than the national rate, states like Colorado and Iowa have rates less than one-third the national level. Given the range of gun homicide rates in the United States, do we really learn very much by comparing a rate for *anything*, particularly something as complicated as gun homicide from a large, diverse country of more than 300 million people, as opposed to small, relatively homogeneous countries like Switzerland, Austria or even the U.K.?

Presenting gun data on a national basis which hides such great regional or ethnic disparities is more troubling when one considers the fact that it is the research of public health scholars like Hemenway which is then utilized by public policy experts and advocates to create and promote legislative and legal remedies for issues like gun violence. I am reminded, for example, of the explosion of rhetoric a few years ago about America's obesity problem, which was described as a "national" health crisis and was often cited as one of the major issues that would have to be addressed in any substantial reorganization of the health care system, such as what happened after 2008 with the planning and implementation of the ACA. Yet while the national obesity figures showed the "average" American to be more than 20% overweight, this figure, like the national numbers on gun homicides, hid significant regional disparities to the point that some states showed little, if any real obesity in their populations, whereas others showed obesity levels often 50% higher than the national average. Based on those numbers, would it have been reasonable to develop one, single response to obesity, or would it have been more advisable to look at the issue regionally, culturally, etc., and come up with more specific plans to deal with the issue relative to where and how it manifested itself in different populations? The same could be said about dealing with guns.

The same type of problem emerges from Hemenway's summary when one looks at the question of what types of weapons are involved in the commission of gun violence. The review article mentions at the beginning that not only do Americans own more guns than the residents of any other advanced country, but in particular they own many more handguns. This is the last time that Hemenway differentiates between types of weapons, and it is a differentiation which, unfortunately, is too often missed or ignored in the public health research that Hemenway so ably summarizes for his readers. The fact is that more than four-fifths of all gun violence which occurs each year results from the use of a handgun. The FBI data shows that 70% of all gun felonies involve the use of a handgun, but this proportion reflects the fact that nearly 20% of gun felonies reported to the FBI do not contain an actual description of the weapon, either because it wasn't found at the scene, or the reporting-recording process didn't pick it up, or some other reason. But why should the percentage of unknown guns be any different than the percentage of known weapons? And if that's the case, which it surely is, then handguns become minimally four-fifths of all gun felony weapons, and I suspect the percentage to be even higher. During the 2013 debate over the New

York SAFE law, which placed strong restrictions on the ownership of so-called assault weapons, the New York State Police reported that gun crimes involved the use of handguns more than 95% of the time.

Most of the public health scholars whose work Hemenway summarizes in his article pay scant or no attention to this issue, simply using the nomenclature "guns" to describe every type of weapon whose presence or use forms the basis for their research. This lack of clarity (or granularity) has the unfortunate consequence of tying the reduction of gun violence to greater controls on all guns which, by definition, make the controls less viable and enforceable (because they have to cover a much greater number of guns), as well as less palatable to gun owners who, in many cases, may not even possess the types of weapons that figure in just about every kind of gun crime.

One of the reasons that public health researchers do not differentiate between types of guns is because the data they use for their research also doesn't attempt to make distinctions in this respect. For example, Hemenway uses as his comparison for states with high gun ownership to states with low gun ownership the very comprehensive surveys conducted by the Behavioral Risk Factor Surveillance System of the CDC.[20] This survey, which queries more than

200,000 households about risk factors for health and health care, included a question about gun ownership in surveys conducted between 2002 and 2004. Yet the fact that they did not differentiate between long guns and hand guns makes the findings substantially less useful in trying to understand patterns of gun ownership or attempting to craft gun control policies that might reduce gun violence or gun crime. This is particularly important because of the extent to which current gun sales are increasingly a function of demand for handguns, but we have no idea whether this reflects older shooters adding new types of weapons to their personal arsenals, or new shooters getting into the game for the first time and being influenced by the gun industry's promotion of assault-style and self-defense weapons.

The biggest issue I have with public health research into the social utility of guns, however, is the inability to forge a definitive causal link between levels of violence and the existence of guns. The problem, as I stated earlier, lies in the inability of researchers to create research scenarios that can control for the absence of guns in environments where guns currently exist; i.e., will the amount of gun violence currently recorded in a particular environment change if the guns are no longer present? This is the assumption, after all, behind every scheme designed to control access to guns, based on the notion that more guns equals more crime.

The way that public health researchers currently approach this issue is to compare behaviors between two populations, one with guns and one without guns, to see if the outcomes vis-à-vis gun use remain the same or change. The best-known work in this regard, summarized in detail by Hemenway, was conducted by Art Kellerman in the early 90's, in which he found differentials both in homicides and suicides between homes that had guns and homes that did not.[21] The problem, of course, was that this approach could not take into account all kinds of social factors that may have influenced certain people to keep guns in their homes, whereas other factors may have militated against other people deciding not to own guns. I happen to think that Kellerman's work is much more substantial and probably more valid than his critics claim it to be, but this still does not erase my concerns about the difficulty of creating a valid "substitution" effect that would help us analyze the impact on the same populations if guns were either not present and then introduced, or were present and then taken away. The inability to create and implement such a research methodology is invariably used by pro-gun advocates to diminish or dismantle public policies that would seek to limit access to guns.

What now follows is an attempt, albeit somewhat haphazardly, to arrive at some kind of causal relationship between violent crime and access or non-access to guns based on FBI data from the 1933 and 1934 UCR reports, which are part of a series beginning in1930, the first UCR ever published by the FBI.[22] The data is somewhat fragmentary and I have to assume that its preparation was not subject to the same degree of analytical rigor that allegedly characterizes the current UCR publications. Furthermore, the national data was aggregated from police departments which represented 54 million out of a total population in 1930 of more than 122 million; in other words, roughly 45% of the country's population, whereas the current UCR aggregates reports from agencies that cover more than 90% of the US. In addition to representing less than half the US population, the 1933 report did not include data from either New York City, Louisville, Atlanta or Memphis, and it is not clear whether these cities furnished data for 1934.

Notwithstanding the differences in the representativeness of the data, violent crime, particularly homicide, shows some interesting parallels between the two periods. In particular, the age distribution for homicides is similar, with homicide perpetrators in the 1930's and the 1980's-90's peaking between the ages of 18 and 24. Racial groupings also show a degree of African-American involvement as homicide perpetrators far beyond their proportion within the overall population. In 1933-34 African-Americans accounted for about 34% of all homicide perpetrators while African-Americans constituted less than 10% of the overall population, whereas whites accounted for 60% of all homicide perpetrators in a country that was 88% white. Comparing the two populations in the 1930's and the 1980's-90's we get the following results:

1930's

Race	Population	Homicide Rate (100K)
White	89.8	5.1
Black	9.7	29.5

1980's-1990's

Race	Population	Homicide Rate (100K)
White	82%	4.5
Black	12%	34.4

What we see from a comparison of the data is that the Black-White disparity in homicide was almost as pronounced in the 1930's as it was in the 1980's-90's. But here is the big difference: guns, particularly handguns, were simply not part of the urban landscape during the 1930's. On the other hand, African-American homicides occurred almost as frequently then as now. Notwithstanding the arbitrary nature of the 1930's data, as well as its limitations in terms of representativeness and other factors, this nevertheless represents an attempt to validate the link between guns and violence through a substitution mechanism (i.e., guns were just not available in the 1930's the way they are available today), and the link doesn't work. I am not arguing that one can entirely separate the issue of violence from the existence of guns. What I am saying is that this comparison, as timid as it is, suggests that guns may play the same role in contemporary violence defined as homicide that they play in suicide, namely, that they are used out of convenience but not out of necessity. If they didn't exist, the factors that promote violence might still be there and people who choose to commit violence would just find another way. In this respect one can argue that guns do represent a negative social utility, but eliminating them would not necessarily eliminate the violent behavior or results of that behavior which today are associated with and, it is assumed, driven by access to guns.

This brings us to the other side of Hemenway's article, namely, the summary of research that shows a positive utility from gun ownership, either in the form of a deterrence that keeps crimes from taking place, or as a self-defense mechanism before or during the commission of the crime itself. As far as gun ownership as a deterrence, Hemenway summarizes research that was done to compare crime rates before and after various communities either required or eliminated gun ownership and he concludes that there is no statistical validity or even causal connection between crime rates and either the presence or absence of legally-owned guns.

As for thwarting actual crimes, Hemenway discusses the available data on the use of guns for self-defense, looking at three sources: police reports, surveys of individuals who claimed to have used guns to thwart crimes before the crimes actually occurred, and surveys of individuals who used guns to protect themselves during or after a crime was committed against them. In brief he finds all of these sources to be insufficient to determine the true degree to which guns can be effectively used in self-defense; hence, he is unable to make any judgment on the positive social utility of gun ownership. The only study based on police reports covered only "unwanted entry" into homes, which could hardly be classified as comprehensive information. As for the use of a gun to prevent a crime from happening that had not yet actually occurred, Hemenway is being polite when he characterizes the answers to such questions as "ambiguous." Finally, the data on gun defense by crime victims, which comes from the National Crime

Victims Survey, appears to indicate a positive social utility in response to certain property crimes, but a neutral or negative social utility when used in response to violent crime insofar as other self-defense methods (leaving the scene, etc.) are utilized with greater success to prevent the victim from being injured in the course of the crime.

Hemenway's article is based on the most comprehensive bibliography assembled as of that date, and if you want to learn what we know and what we don't know about guns, the people who use guns and the way guns are used, I suggest you read through this list. Having done so, I can state without equivocation that his summary of the two sides of the debate is balanced and fair. To be sure, in his own research he has consistently argued for the negative social utility of guns, but this article cannot be construed as advancing that position in any biased or prejudicial way. The fact that he devotes more than twice as much space to a summary of the negative social utility literature as is given over to the positive viewpoint is a function of the fact that so much more research has been published on the former, notwithstanding the degree to which the conclusions of the latter argument tend to hold the public sway.

The biggest problem in both defining and understanding the argument over the social utility of guns is that the two sides aren't really barking up the same tree. The negative argument begins with the premise that guns are inherently dangerous, that regardless of what is done with them, *ipso facto* they constitute a risk. As a result, virtually all of the negative social utility research focuses on measuring the degree of risk posed by the existence and/or use of guns. The risk may be greater or smaller depending on what is being measured, but the risk is generic to the issue that is being measured, not determined by the results of the measurement.

On the other side of the argument, the positive social utility researchers begin with the assumption that guns do not represent any real risk at all. And to the extent that there is any risk, as defined by an insignificant amount of unintentional injury, this cannot stand against the degree to which gun ownership confers positive social utility not just on the owners of the guns, but on society as a whole. After all, as people like Kleck argue, when a person carrying a gun thwarts a crime by defensively brandishing the weapon, the individual who otherwise might have committed a crime may think twice before going up against his next potential victim, thus resulting in less harm to persons beyond the one who was actually carrying a gun. When crime rates drop in a community because the law allows people to carry concealed weapons whether they do or not, everyone benefits from less crime, not just the individuals walking around with a gun.

The problem with the positive social utility argument is that researchers on that side of the fence are using gun access to explain behavioral change that may have nothing at all to do with guns or access to guns. The research by Kleck has no real value in terms of establishing causal connections between carrying a gun and thwarting possible crimes because he could not establish whether an actual crime might have occurred if any one of the 213 respondents with whom he completed a valid interview could verify that without the existence of a gun in their hands a crime would have taken place. As for the other major "more guns = less crime" proponent, John Lott, most of the crime decline that he claimed to have followed from increased issuance of CCW permits actually took place before CCW became, generally speaking, the law of the land, whereas crime rates stabilized and in some places increased with the issuance of more CCW. Furthermore, Lott assumed that just as more guns = less crime, so more CCW = more guns being carried around. Yet he has never made any effort to test whether or not this assumption is true.

Despite the fact that the overwhelming bulk of the public health research summarized by Hemenway points towards a general consensus of the negative social utility of guns, it has to be said that, from a practical standpoint, the results of the research has moved the argument about guns in the other direction. In the notes to his summary, Hemenway cites five articles or books that support the positive social utility of guns, and more than ninety studies that come down on the negative side of the coin. In other words, over the last two decades, researchers who are trying to figure out the role that guns really play in American society believe that the role is basically negative by a ratio of twenty to one.

You would think that such an extraordinary research consensus over a twenty-year period would result in laws and regulations covering guns that reflected this negative point of view, right? Wrong. As opposed to public health research on risks like smoking or auto safety, legislators at both the state and federal levels responded to the findings of researchers on both topics by instituting programs and policies designed to lessen harm caused by smoking among children and driving around without restraints, again aimed primarily at youth and young adults. In the case of guns, on the other hand, the development of a research consensus on the health risks posed by guns has emerged at exactly the same time that virtually every state legislature gave residents the virtually unregulated ability to walk around with a gun, while at the federal level guns were exempted from consumer protection and liability laws during the Bush II administration, and of course the SCOTUS ruled that the 2nd Amendment allowed Americans to keep loaded and unlocked guns in their homes for self-defense. How and why has such a divergence between research and reality taken place? The answers to this question will occupy the final two chapters of this book.

CHAPTER 5

ENTER THE SCIENTISTS

Public policy usually begins with a Task Force. You get the best and brightest together, start the meeting with a nice lunch, and then proceed to come up with a plan to put together a report on whatever issue the Task Force was created to analyze and discuss. In theory, the report of the Task Force will become the basis for whatever public policy might be developed in response to the issue whose solution the Task Force was created to find. In reality, the job of the Task Force is to collect whatever documentation might exist on a particular problem, engage some experts to review the documentation, and then issue a report. Such an activity was conducted as regards the issue of gun violence in 2001-2002 and resulted in the publication of a book, *Firearms and Violence, A Critical Review,* in 2005.[1]

The Task Force in this instance was actually the Committee To Improve Research Information And Data On Firearms, which was convened by the

National Research Council of the National Academies of Sciences, the federally-chartered, "self-perpetuating society of distinguished scholars engaged in scientific and engineering research, dedicated to the furtherance of science and technology and to their use for the general welfare." Whew. More than 500 Nobel prize winners are members of the Academies, and their research spans the scientific horizon from global warming, to biological dangers, to treatment of returning war veterans, to the issue of guns. It was to this organization that President Obama turned in 2013 after Sandy Hook and asked for advice on gun violence research priorities which, a year after the report was issued, have yet to be funded by the CDC. But let's come back to the 2013 report a little later on. Right now I want to stick with the volume published in 2005, based on a series of meetings and discussions that took place in 2001-2002.

The importance of this effort for understanding the ins and outs of the gun debate lies in the fact that by the time it was published, the major research on the social utility of guns had already appeared. In fact, the work of scholars like Kleck, Lott and Hemenway, reviewed in Chapter 2, 3 and 4 of this book, was the focus of discussion and analysis by the Committee whose basic approach, whether they knew it or not, was to review the arguments for the positive and negative social utility of guns and decide which argument bore more fruit. To further its work, the Committee held four public hearings, what they referred to as workshops, and heard from more than 40 individuals who represented the entire spectrum of pro-gun and anti-gun researchers, including Kleck, Lott, Hemenway, staff from the NRA, the Brady Campaign, the ATF, and just about anyone and everyone else whose views on this subject needed to be taken into account. In other words, although most of the people whose testimony was ultimately analyzed by the Committee could not in any way, shape or form be considered scientists, nobody was going to be able to criticize the National Research Council for creating any kind of bias in their report based on the backgrounds and viewpoints of the people whose presentations would form the conclusions on which the report was based. Again, whew.

In this regard it's instructive to take a look at the background and professional activities of the Committee members, beginning with the Chair, Charles Wellford. Now Emeritus at the University of Maryland, Wellford was long-time Chair of the Department of Criminology and, according to his c.v., specialized in sentencing, crime measurement and policing. Over the years he has evidently served on just about every Federal commission and committee for anything having to do with criminal administration, in particular administration related to data technology and data services. Given the fact that his campus is located just outside of Washington D.C., it's understandable why he would focus much of his career energies on public service related to criminology and criminal justice; after all, why fly someone in from the West Coast when you have an expert sitting a stone's throw away from every Federal agency responsible for crime and enforcement? The fact that Wellford's expertise lies in the area of criminal data is also relevant insofar as the purpose of the Academy's gun initiative was to analyze gaps in "research information and data."

In addition to Wellford, the Committee's membership and study directors consisted of 16 academics, of whom the majority were criminologists, along with several economists, psychologists and psychiatrists and one physician, a pediatrician from the New Jersey Medical School who, like Wellford, has served on endless committees, policy boards, etc., etc., etc. The two luminaries on the Committee, so to speak, were John Q. Wilson and Steven Levitt, the former known primarily for his "broken windows" thesis of crime control, which is credited with the development of aggressive, in-your-face policing in

New York and elsewhere; and the latter known best as the author of *Freakonomics*, and in criminology circles, for a provocative but never-validated theory about the relationship between legalized abortion and decline of crime.[2]

The approach taken by the Committee was not dissimilar to what Hemenway would later do in his 2007 summary article that compared negative to positive social utility of guns, namely, the Committee examined the validity of the data used to draw conclusions about gun violence, up to and including attempting replication analyses of the raw data itself. The Committee looked at Kleck and Lott's work, in terms of their arguments promoting "more guns = less crime"; they also examined public health research on access to guns relative to rates of crime and suicides, and also looked at the value of formal (police) and informal (grass-roots) efforts to reduce gun crime. I'll start with the conclusion and then go into the details. Bottom line: the data on gun violence, no matter what specific issue is measured, was insufficient to come to any definitive conclusions about what to do about guns. That is to say, neither the positive nor the negative social value of guns could be established by the National Academy, nor could it be determined whether any particular intervention made a difference when it came to reducing gun violence.

Before we get into the details of the Committee's work, it is important to establish the framework in which the Committee was established and proceeded about its business. This is the reason that I described the backgrounds of all Committee members, whose approach to the issue must be examined in order to understand both what they were looking to learn, as well as their conclusions as to what they learned. The fact that there was not a single member of the Committee with a background or c.v. in the public health approach to gun violence is a very telling issue in judging the value of the Committee's overall work. A majority of the members were academic criminologists whose research specialties, for the most part, had little connection to the issue of guns. Furthermore, the fact that they came to the subject from a criminological background would make them perhaps more sensitive to the methodological shortcomings of the research that framed arguments within a crime perspective, but less concerned with much of the public health research which, in many if not most cases, focused marginally, if at all on issues about guns and crime. The research by Kleck and Lott which supports the positive social utility argument about guns relies overwhelmingly on criminological data and methodology; the research which supports the negative social utility argument rarely even uses criminal evidence to makes its case. This is a fundamental dichotomy in the whole corpus of gun research which the Committee never even acknowledged, either in its summary or in the detailed examination of the scholarly artifacts of gun research.

But back to the details. In the words of the Committee:

> "There is hardly a more contentious issue in American society than the ownership of firearms and various proposals for their control. [p. 11] Given the importance of this issue and the continued controversy surrounding the debate on firearms, the need was clear for an unbiased assessment of the existing portfolio of data and research. [p. 13] All research must follow some basic standards to be accepted by the community of scholars in a field—firearms research is no different. These standards are well known to scientists:
>
> - Pose significant questions that can be investigated empirically.
> - Link research to relevant theory.
> - Use methods that permit direct investigation of the question.

- Provide a coherent and explicit chain of reasoning.
- Replicate and generalize across studies.
- Disclose research to encourage professional scrutiny and critique.

While any group of scholars might modify this list, it poses some commonly accepted standards that our committee used to begin its evaluation of the literature of firearm violence."[3]

So here is the approach taken by the National Academy to determine the value of research conducted on gun violence and to identify existing gaps in the research that still needed to be filled. And how well did the two sides arguing about the social utility of guns do when the experts applied the criteria for judging their work as listed above? Not very well, I'm afraid, not very well. Let's start with the analysis of the positive social utility arguments, i.e., Kleck and Lott.

In the case of Kleck, the Academy first noted the great disparity between his estimates of 2.5 million DGUs annually versus the less than 100,000 DGUs derived from the surveys conducted by the NCVS. They surmised that the primary cause of this disparity "is the disagreement over the definition of defensive gun use—in particular, whether it should be defined as a response to victimization or as a means to prevent victimization from occurring in the first place."[4] After reviewing all the literature, the Academy concludes that "fundamental problems in defining what is meant by defensive gun use may be a primary impediment to accurate measurement."[5]

In addition to examining the Kleck argument that posited millions of DGUs each year, the Committee also analyzed the arguments of Kleck's critics, in particular the whole question of inaccurate reporting based either on faulty memory, mistaken perceptions about what really happened, and the difficulty of deriving any generalized information about what, in reality, is a "rare event." While recognizing the difficulties in accepting the results of any sampling survey as representative of the population in general, the Committee could not definitively come down either for or against the validity of Kleck's work, calling instead for a "systematic and rigorous" program to eliminate uncertainties in the current DGU arguments.

If the Committee truly believed that they subjected Kleck's work to their own criteria for judging the validity of arguments about DGUs, then either they didn't read his work or they ignored their own criteria for judging its validity. Note above their statement that the research has to "provide a clear and coherent chain of reasoning." How could the Committee not have picked up the fact that Kleck's entire survey was based on an initial question which provided no coherent chain of reasoning at all? Here was the question: "Have you yourself or another member of your household used a gun, even if it was not fired for self-protection or for the protection of property at home, work or elsewhere?"[6] If the individual who answered the phone answered in the affirmative, the interview continued; if the answer was a negative, the interview ended at that point.

If Kleck were really interested in scientifically establishing whether access to guns thwarted what otherwise would have been the commission of a crime, the respondent should have then been asked to explain how or why he/she believed that a crime was about to take place. They were not asked to validate their belief in the possible commission of a crime against them in any way. The Commission went on for page after page explaining that it had difficulty accepting the variance of DGU numbers between Kleck's survey and the surveys conducted by the NCVS; a variance it claimed was due to a lack of consistent definitions about what constituted a DGU. But how about the issue of what constituted a crime?

On this issue the Committee's more than 7,000-word discussion about Kleck's work was totally and completely silent.

But let's go further into this issue of a "coherent chain of reasoning" which the Committee claimed was absolutely essential for determining the scientific validity of the work it received and reviewed. The Committee accepted without question Kleck's approach to defining DGU behavior as making a distinction between "offensive" gun use on the one hand and "defensive" gun use on the other. Accordingly, offensive gun use which results in an incomplete or criminal attack is separated from defensive gun use which results in no attack.[7] This distinction, which was accepted unstintingly by the Committee, is reproduced here:

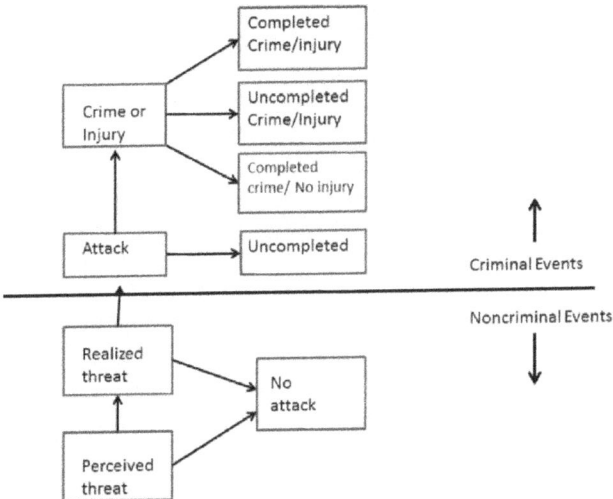

Now compare this diagram to a similar diagram which, for purposes of discussion, I have edited by adding a dotted, vertical line with captions at the bottom of the illustration:

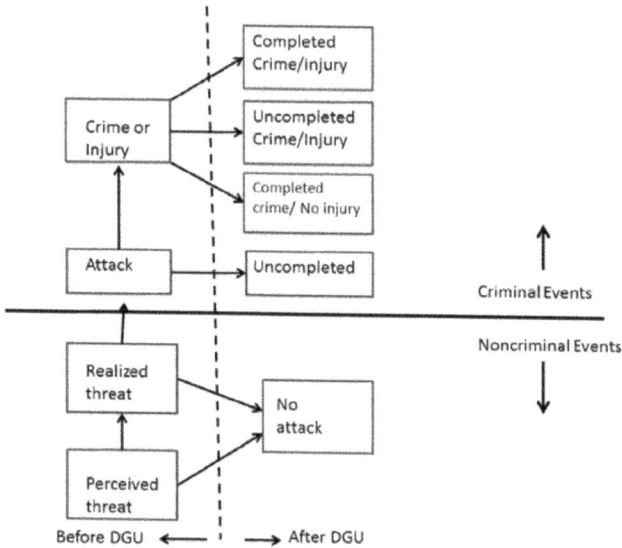

Kleck's argument for the multi-million DGUs that take place each year is based solely on a survey which found that a certain number of respondents claimed to have used guns against what they believed was a "perceived threat." In other words, the survey and the data which it furnished was based on respondents making a positive response to a question about a "perceived threat" which then resulted in no crime taking place (lowest box in first diagram). No attempt was made to decode their answers in such a way as to validate whether, in fact, they might have been placed in any of the other categories, either in terms of what happened before the DGU allegedly took place, or during or after it took place.

How can such a methodology be even remotely considered as reflecting a "coherent" chain of reasoning? It cannot, and here's the reason: if we are to believe Kleck's results, we have to assume that *every single DGU that was reported in his survey resulted in a crime not taking place.* After all, he asked respondents whether they or other family members "used" a gun to protect themselves or their property from a crime that had not yet taken place. Does this mean that because the individual whose presence provoked Kleck's interview subject to pull out a gun was intent on committing a crime? Was the "proof" of his criminal intent the fact that when he saw a gun he turned and ran away? Is there anyone out there who wouldn't run away if he was suddenly confronted by someone brandishing a gun?

But that's not the entire problem with Kleck. The bigger problem lies in the assumptions which underlie the diagram in which he differentiates between "offensive" and "defensive" gun use. Note that he assumes a dichotomy between "defensive" and "offensive" gun use based on the intent of the user. The defensive gun user is engaged in a "noncriminal" event; the offensive gun user is engaged in a "criminal" event. This scenario assumes that the entire event occurred because someone who intended to commit a crime walked up to someone else who then defended himself/herself against the crime that otherwise would have taken place.

Which is all fine and well for fiction, but that's not how things happen in the real world. In the real world, in the world where guns are pulled out and used for whatever reason they are used, the moment at which the "attacker" learns that the "victim" has a gun doesn't come up out of nowhere. I don't walk down the street with a gun in my pocket and when someone comes up to me and appears to be about to attack me I then show him the gun and off he runs. In the real world we know each other, we have had contact with one another, we have had an argument, maybe it's escalated to a fistfight, maybe even worse. This is the real world, this is the world that is reflected in the revised diagram of Kleck's scenario, and this is the world that the questions in Kleck's survey didn't reflect at all. How is it possible, for example, that Kleck didn't ask a single respondent whether he or she knew their assailant prior to the alleged DGU when the incidence of prior familiarity between criminal and victim in aggravated assaults runs 80% or higher? And how is it that the

Committee's team of expert reviewers could have read Kleck's work and not singled this omission out as basically invalidating his research as a whole? After all, the Committee was comprised primarily of criminologists. None of them ever read anything by a guy named Wolfgang?

Kleck's DGU research is so lacking in context and is so far removed from the reality of criminal activity as to strain credibility and the whole notion of a scientific method. The point is that the scenario created by Kleck in which DGUs are noncriminal events which can never flow over into criminal events is not how things really happen. And therefore to announce that a certain type of behavior that is based on such unreal assumptions occurs millions of times is to announce that something happens millions of times that may have never happened at all. The problem with the criticisms of Kleck, both by the Committee and by other scholars whose criticisms are discussed by the Committee, is that they focus on the statistical methodology employed by Kleck to analyze his survey results. Which is all fine and well, except that it's not the statistics that are flawed. It's the basic assumptions that Kleck used to create his survey, assumptions that were either accepted by the Committee or not discussed by the Committee at all.

The Committee did the same number when it reviewed the work of John Lott which, as I discussed in Chapter 3, took Kleck's argument a step further and attempted to tie the issuance of concealed-carry permits to overall declines in crime. The first problem that confronted the Committee, whose consulting experts tried to replicate Lott's results, was that they couldn't get the actual data from Lott who claimed that it was "lost." This claim, and the attempts to invalidate Lott completely on that basis or allow for the substitution of similar data, has created a veritable cottage industry within the field of gun studies in and all by itself. I'm not going to waste your time reviewing the ins and outs of this controversy, except to note that the Committee acknowledged and then made no further comment about it in a statement that took up exactly one footnote in the more than thirty pages devoted to Lott's work.

I would be more sanguine about the fact that Lott was unable to provide his original data, nor would it bother me that his work has never appeared in any publication that could remotely pass muster as using a peer-review method to determine the suitability of publishing it, were it not for two facts. Fact #1 is that Lott's work, even more than the work by Gary Kleck, has been used again and again by pro-gun politicians to promote concealed-carry laws both in individual states and the country as a whole. Fact #2 is that the Committee not only dismissed criticisms of Lott's loss of data by scholars because they held "a priori beliefs or expectations" that were contrary to Lott's conclusions (a polite way of saying that they were prejudiced against Lott), but also directed readers to Lott's own defense of his work without even taking the trouble to figure out whether what Lott said to defend himself was true.

Not only did the Committee dismiss criticisms of Lott's work by other scholars, they went even further to defend him in their comment about the substitute data that Lott provided for them to review. Here's what they said: "The committee was unable to replicate Lott's estimate of the reduction in the murder rate, although the estimates are close and consistent with the conclusion that right-to-carry laws reduce the incidence of murder. *Through communication with Lott* [my italics], the committee learned that the data used to construct Table 4.1 of Lott [reference to his 2000 publication] were lost and that the data supplied to the committee *are a reconstruction and not necessarily identical to the original data.*"[8] [again my italics]

What are they talking about? This is a committee of the National Academy of Sciences? This is a committee of the organization whose mission is to "further science in America"? This is a committee which announced at the beginning of this study that it would examine research which, among other things, would use "methods that permit direct investigation of the question"? And what method did they choose to use in examining Lott's work? After they informed him that the data he sent them could not be replicated to support his findings, they gave him the opportunity to send them a different set of data! And they call their work an "unbiased assessment of the existing portfolio of research" on gun violence?

I have no choice at this point but to interject an editorial comment. Remember Ayatollah Khomeni? He was the exiled religious leader who returned to Iran in 1980 following the departure of the Shah and led the Iranian government until his death in in 1989. I recall that several months before his return to Iran, he broadcast a speech from his headquarters outside of Paris in which he referred to the United States government as the "Great Satan." When I heard this remark it occurred to me that an entirely new nomenclature had just been injected into world political discourse, one for which we had neither experience nor precedent in terms of how to respond.

Now I'm not saying that the report on gun violence published by the National Academy should be considered in any way, shape or form to hold the slightest importance next to the revolution that overthrew the Shah and inaugurated a new chapter in international relations beginning in 1979. But I did have something of the selfsame reaction to the gun control report when I read the sentence above in which the Committee simply allowed Lott to send them a "revised" version of the data whose results could not be validated based on what he had previously sent them to review.

But in the interests of science and objectivity, I decided to hold my water and wait to read the conclusions that the Committee made when it came to judging the overall validity of Lott's work. And here is what the Committee decided to say:

> The literature on right-to-carry laws summarized in this chapter has obtained conflicting estimates of their effects on crime. The initial model specification, when extended to new data [the data that Lott gave the Committee after he admitted that the previous data wasn't, shall we say, necessarily authentic] does not show evidence that passage of right-to-carry laws reduces crime. Thus, the Committee concludes that *with the current evidence* [my italics] it is not possible to determine that there is a causal link between the passage of right-to-carry laws and crime rates."[9]

In other words, if Lott is wrong, so is everyone else. A point which the Committee stated explicitly at the end of this chapter when they concluded, "If further headway is to be made on this question, new analytical models and data sets will have to be used."[10]

So maybe what the Committee is hoping is that Lott will invent a third dataset that can be used to make "further headway" on this issue. Meanwhile, the fact that the Committee chose to dedicate this entire issue to a search for whether concealed-carry laws reduce crime doesn't alter a fundamental bias in their approach to the question, because they chose to build the entire chapter around Lott's argument that more CCW equals less crime. But what if the chapter had instead been built around the idea that more CCW results in *more* crime?

This is the argument made by two researchers, Ian Ayres and John Donohue, who, using Lott's own data, first published a peer-reviewed article in 1999 and followed this with a much more detailed article published in 2003.[11] The second piece, which runs 100 pages and could qualify as a small book, was cited by the Committee as resulting in estimates of declining crime that were not "statistically significant," i.e., could not be used to substantially revise Lott. On the other hand, when the Committee used the "revised, new data" given to them by Lott, they still could not replicate his findings but "exactly replicated" the results reported by Ayres and Donohue. So a book whose main thesis argues that giving people CCWs and letting them walk around with a gun decreases crime gets blown into a national screed that is used by the gun industry to promote the social utility of guns, but a detailed and lengthy article that argues exactly the reverse is given a few sentences in an Academy of Science report which notes that the former book contains data that cannot be replicated using the author's statistical model, but the latter work contains a different statistical approach which allows the same data to tell a very different and valid tale. I know you just read a very long sentence, but the bottom line is that Ayres and Donohue used the data provided by Lott to validate exactly the reverse argument from his, but somehow the Committee missed the whole point.

The point is that the article by Ayres and Donohue is not just a critique of Lott's work, even though its title, *Shooting Down the "More Guns, Less Crime" Hypothesis*, certainly leads the unwary reader to believe this is the case. In fact, the article is a very clear argument for the notion that, in a majority of jurisdictions which issued concealed-carry permits, the increase in CCW was coincident with either no decline or an increase in overall violent crime in the period *after* these jurisdictions adopted shall-issue CCW laws. Granted, the work by Ayres and Donohue was written in the context of critiquing John Lott, and granted many of the ambiguities and limitations of data and analysis pointed out by the Committee with reference to Lott's work apply to the work of Ayres and Donohue as well. But in terms of informing and influencing public policy and/or the public debate about guns, it's one thing to say that the expansion of CCW does not appear to be a factor in Americans experiencing less crime; it's quite another to argue that the more people going around armed, the more crime seems to occur. The fact that the Committee arbitrarily chose to examine this issue from the perspective created by Lott's approach negated the essential value and importance of Ayres and Donohue's work. In effect, what the Committee managed to accomplish in this section of the report was to elevate the importance of Lott's work relative to the national debate, and diminish the importance of the contrary point of view. Thanks.

What did Ayres and Donohue discover about the relationship between CCW and rates of crime? Basically, by shifting the analysis to a longer chronology, they found that in a majority of jurisdictions, the issuing of shall-issue CCW was coterminous not with a decline in violent crime, but in an increase in every crime category, along with a net increase in the dollar cost of crime, rather than a savings, per the argument by Lott. As to crime rates, "Overall, there are almost twice as many jurisdictions with an estimated increase in violent crime (fifteen) as those with an estimated decrease (nine)."[12] As for the costs of crime decreasing, which was a major argument by Lott about the positive social utility of guns, this study found that the "net annual impact … was to increase the dollar harm of crime by approximately $1 billion,"[13] a far different number than the annual $5 billion savings estimated by Lott.

Notwithstanding the different results of shall-issue CCW found by Lott on the one hand and Ayres and Donohue on the other, there is a much larger problem about this entire subject which the Committee never thought to mention at all. And this has to do with the criminological underpinnings of Lott's approach having nothing to do with the use or abuse of the statistical data itself. And while Ayres and Donohue did not really discuss this problem in the 2003 article that we summarized above, they discussed it in detail in a previous article published in 1999 which the Committee chose not to mention at all. In this earlier article, Ayres and Donohue addressed the underlying assumptions about criminal behavior which Lott used to explain the different crime trends he found in jurisdictions whose issuance of CCW and the resultant change in criminality formed the basis of his book.

In brief, Lott argued for what could be called a "substitution" effect; i.e., that as criminals perceived the possibility that more of their potential victims might be armed, they tended to shift away from crimes which resulted in face-to-face contact with victims and replaced such criminality with crimes where the absence of a victim allowed the crime to take place. He argued this point because in a majority of states where he found a decline in violent crime after the adoption of CCW, these same jurisdictions experienced higher levels of property crime, a decline of 5% in violent crimes being partially offset by a 2.7% increase in property crimes, particularly auto theft and larceny.[14]

And here is where, as far as I am concerned, Lott's entire thesis should have been thrown out. Not because he failed to inform the Committee that the data he first gave them was purloined, not because the Committee was unable to replicate the analytical results using Lott's data and his methodology, but because his understanding or, I should say, his lack of understanding about criminality and criminology is simply immense. It flies so far away from reality and from overwhelming scholarly evidence, much of it produced by criminologists who are as politically conservative as Lott, that I simply fail to see how a committee of scientists whose mission is to advance science and inform the country from a scientific perspective could even consider evaluating his work. And remember that these scientists were, after all, mostly criminologists. To their credit, as I mentioned above, Ayres and Donohue picked up this issue in their 1999 review of Lott's book, but chose to move away from it in the paper they published in 2003. But I would like to return to it because it is ultimately not only indicative of the mind-set of the community which preaches the positive social utility of guns, but explains in many respects the extreme degree of division separating the two sides in the gun debate today.

Behind Lott's approach to the alleged connection between CCW and crime rates is the assumption that the world can be neatly divided into two groups: good people and bad people, or the way Wayne LaPierre puts it, good guys and bad guys. The good people are law-abiding, the bad people commit crimes. The good people need to protect themselves from criminals, the bad people need to find ways to commit criminal acts for which they won't be caught or won't suffer penalties or injuries. Not only can we construct a typology in which we separate "good" from "bad," but we can also assume that the two groups know what the other is doing and react to what the other does in premeditated and calculated ways. Hence, Lott finds that while issuance of CCW results in a decrease in violent crime, it also results in an increase in property crime because criminals understand that committing a property crime means a smaller chance of confronting the victim face-to-face and therefore a smaller chance of being wounded or killed if the intended victim is carrying a gun.

The problem with this, as pointed out by Ayres and Donahue, is that it's a fanciful and wholly inaccurate approach to understanding the commission of crimes. First of all, violent crime is impulsive and, with the exception of robbery, is usually an event of the moment which has little, if anything to do with any kind of premeditated design. Second, and more important, when we come to criminal assaults, particularly homicides, the criminal act is not only overwhelmingly impulsive, but in the words of the foremost scholar of homicide, "the victim is often a major contributor to the criminal act."[15] Given the reality of violent criminal behavior, not the fantasy as concocted by Lott, it is simply absurd to produce an entire analytical work whose explanation for its results rests on the idea that if criminals believe that the non-criminals are walking around armed, they will consciously choose to substitute another form of criminal behavior, such as car theft, in which the odds of encountering another real person go down.

Lott has continued to beat the drums for this entirely manufactured vision of criminal behavior by serving as the NRA's chief spear carrier in its campaign to rid America of "gun-free" zones. The whole notion of designating certain properties as being areas where guns cannot be transported or stored was embodied first and foremost in the Gun-Free School Zones Act of 1990 that was signed into law by George Bush. Basically the law does not allow individuals to bring a gun onto school property unless they have a license which enables them to carry a weapon on their person, concealed or not, regardless of where they decide to go. The NRA has always opposed such laws because this contradicts their strategy of promoting armed citizens as the first line of defense against crime. Lott argues against gun-free zones every chance he gets, and since he is frequently a media guest on various Fox outlets, he gets plenty of opportunities to vent his opinions, based on facts or not. Usually not.

Several months after the movie theater mass shooting in Aurora, he posted a commentary on his website in which he claimed that the shooter, James Holmes, had chosen the particular theater because it was the only one near his residence that did not allow patrons to bring concealed guns. There has never been a single statement by anyone involved in the Holmes shooting indicating why he went into the Cinemark and shot 12 people dead. But Lott figured it out. He has also claimed that civilians with concealed weapons "have prevented mass shootings on many occasions."[16] In fact, over the last 30 years it appears to be the case that not a single shooting where four or more people died was then stopped by a civilian carrying a gun.[17] The FBI recently issued a report covering 160 "active shootings" between 2000 and 2013. The term "active shootings" is defined as shootings in which both law enforcement personnel *and citizens* [my italics] have the potential to affect the outcome of the event based upon their responses." Know how many of these incidents ended because a "good guy" had a gun? One.

I don't blame Lott for playing fast and loose with the truth. Despite a plethora of data, graphs and charts, he's not a scholar, nor a researcher. He's a promoter and as a promoter basically he can say whatever he wants. The only problem is that when a scholarly committee of the National Academy of Sciences spends a significant portion of their gun violence report discussing his work, this elevates him to the level of scholar and allows him to make claims about the value of his research which simply cannot be considered true. And even though the committee explicitly stated that they could not replicate the results of his work, their conclusion was that all of the research conducted by everyone on the issue of concealed-carry and crime rates needed to be looked at again. Which is another way of telling the positive social utility crowd that they can continue to argue their case because the other side hasn't made a better argument to contradict or disprove what they want to say.

While the committee essentially argued that the research and critiques of positive social utility were both flawed, they were more concerned about the degree to which the entire field of research suffered from a "lack of reliable and valid data." Thus, while existing research had opened up important lines of inquiry, in what the committee termed "key" data areas—the availability, use and role of firearms in injuries and death—the report concluded that "critical information is absent."[18] After summarizing the contents of 34 databases from government and private sources, the committee concluded that the "existing" data did not allow for the answering of such critical questions as:

1. Where do youth who shoot themselves or others obtain their guns?

2. In what proportion of intimate-partner homicides committed with a gun does the offender also take his or her life or the lives of the victim's children or protectors?

3. Did the number of people shot with assault weapons change after the passage of the 1994 ban on assault weapons?

4. What are the most common circumstances leading to unintentional firearm-related deaths? Are particular types of makes and models of firearms overrepresented in unintentional-related deaths?

5. What proportion of suicide or homicide victims were under the care of a mental health professional? What proportion were intoxicated with alcohol or illicit drugs at the time of death? How do these proportions compare with those for suicides committed by other means?[19]

While the committee credits two of the most eminent gun violence researchers for providing these questions, it's not clear to me why the committee believes that only an examination of more data can provide the necessary answers to those questions, nor whether these questions are even relevant to a better understanding of gun violence. Take the first question on how minors acquire guns. In the case of suicides, most teens use guns that they find in their homes, as is the case with just about everyone who uses a gun to end their own life. The data sources cited by the committee don't reveal the actual ownership of guns used in suicides, but you really don't need to be a rocket scientist to figure that one out.

As for teens using guns to commit homicides, or anyone using a gun in a crime, there is simply no way that any comprehensive data showing ownership of crime guns could be created other than through a massive investment of time and money, but there have been endless peer-reviewed studies of how teen and adult criminals get their hands on guns, time-to-crime studies of guns, cost of crime guns and so forth. What is the committee saying? That until we know where kids get guns, we can't definitively state that guns in the hands of minors are a bad thing? I can't find a definitive statement of that sort anywhere in this report. So until we get more data, perhaps it isn't true. After all, this report is based on a scientific approach, right?

As to Question #3 on the effect of the Assault Weapons Ban, we know from the FBI, among other sources, that all types of long guns, not just assault rifles, accounted for a small percentage of gun homicides both before and after the ban was enacted in 1994. The real issue which the committee in its wisdom neglected to mention was the 10-shot magazine capacity limitation that was also part of the

Assault Weapons Ban and may, in fact, have played a role in trends of gun mortality and morbidity, particularly as regards the question of mass or multiple shootings.[20]

As to Question #4 regarding the circumstances surrounding unintentional injuries from guns, this may not be something that would ever be known on any national or even regional scale, but if the committee would like to pursue this question further without benefit of a comprehensive data source or a statistical package to use in analyzing the raw results, let me break the news to them gently. All you have to do to determine the most important circumstance in *all* unintentional shootings is to pick up a gun that isn't loaded, pull the trigger and see if it goes—*boom!* In case you haven't figured it out yet, it won't. Now, it seems to me that if the committee was, as they said, interested in filling up data gaps in order to develop cogent and correct public policies about guns, here's a gap which simply cannot be said to exist. Oh yes, in some abstract, meaningless way the data gap exists if we define it as any question that we choose to ask about guns for which there is not readily available and comprehensive bunch of data that we can tap. But a gun cannot go off if it isn't loaded or, except in rare circumstances, if the trigger isn't pulled, or better yet, a combination of both. This one can't be figured out because we don't have enough data? I beg the committee. Really, you can do better than that.

This report was issued eight years after Congress threw the NRA a bone and voted to defund gun research from the budget of the CDC. In the aftermath of the Assault Weapons Ban and the Brady Bill, both of which Clinton was able to get through Congress in 1994, the NRA needed something to show its membership to prove that it was still intent in protecting their rights, and the CDC funding was a sitting duck; not so much because the termination of gun research would really make a difference in terms of gun regulations per se, but because in the greater scheme of things the actual amount of medical research funding devoted to gun violence was hardly visible in the government's overall spending on public health. And just as small allotments of money have a way of surviving the Congressional budgetary axe because nobody notices they're there, so small amounts of dough can also be made to disappear much more easily because there simply isn't enough interest or a large enough constituency to keep the line item alive. So when a Republican Congressman from Arkansas, Jay Dickey, inserted language in the 1997 CDC budget that explicitly dropped gun research from the CDC agenda, even though Dickey's amendment did not ban gun research by the federal government overall, there was the usual hue and cry from some of the medical associations and other like-minded groups, but the defunding language remained.

Not that research into aspects of gun violence didn't continue with support from other sources. Of the 100+ articles, nearly all of them appearing in peer-reviewed journals whose contents Hemenway summarized in 2007, more than two-thirds appeared after the CDC's gun research was de-funded, and there were many additional published studies that Hemenway chose not to list. This continued effort to collect, aggregate and analyze data about gun violence has not abated since Hemenway summarized the scholarly state of things in 2007, but if anything has increased in scope, largely given to the energies of Hemenway's research center at the Harvard School of Public Health and the gun research efforts which nest in the Johns Hopkins University Bloomberg School of Public Health. A section covering institutional research efforts would not be complete without mentioning the unique work of Garen Wintemute, an emergency room physician in California, who self-funded his own research institute after his CDC support disappeared. Wintemute is not only acknowledged as one of the premier medical researchers in the area of gun violence, but he has combined theoretical analysis with hands-on forays into gun dealerships, gun shows, and even gun manufacturers, to create an original and compelling portrait of guns and gun violence today.[21]

If the National Academy Committee issued its report on gun violence with the hopes that its call for more research might spur a refunding of the CDC, not only was this a flight from reality in terms of possible political scenarios, but the Committee's ultimate finding that much research still needed to be done has little connection to the justifications from a scholarly perspective that would help gun control policies advance either at the state level or with the Feds. After all, we still don't know exactly why cells in lungs begin to multiply when someone fills their lungs with smoke, but we have seen it happen enough times to adopt all kinds of controls over cigarettes in the name of the common good. The scientific rigor that the National Academy applied to judging the validity of gun research is really much more a strategy to let non-researchers like Kleck and Lott off the hook.

What's interesting about the field of gun research is that the arguments made by researchers like Kleck and Lott about the positive social utility of guns appears to have come to an end. Or at least their work has not spawned a significant or even insignificant amount of scholarly literature designed to validate or bolster their points of view. Given the amount spent by conservative think-tanks like the Heritage Foundation or the Cato Institute, you would think that there would be a few enterprising graduate students who would attempt to conduct research that would validate the positive utility approach, or that Kleck and Lott themselves would try to respond to doubts about their research by conducting more studies in kind. Kleck spends a good deal of his time appearing as an expert witness in various courtroom venues where gun control legislation is argued and either affirmed or overturned; Lott has made himself into something of a hyper-conservative commentator on all sorts of issues, many of which have nothing to do with guns.

Meanwhile, although research on guns continued apace even without government funding, there has been a growing dichotomy between the degree to which the peer-reviewed research continues to pile up evidence on the negative side of the social utility argument while public opinion and public policy has continually widened the degree to which Americans gain access to guns in order to use them for positive social ends. In the early 90's, following the publication of the Academy report, only 20 states were considered "shall issue" CCW jurisdictions, meaning that concealed-carry permits were more or less issued automatically to anyone who met the legal qualifications without the requirement to demonstrate some sort of special business or personal need to walk around with a gun. Today there are only 9 states plus the District of Columbia which still issue CCW permits on a strict, case-by-case basis; in other words, at the present time, less than 80 million of the current population of 316 million Americans live in jurisdictions where shall-issue laws are not yet in effect. Furthermore, the 2008 Heller decision definitively clarified the meaning of the 2nd Amendment, defining it as granting gun owners the positive social utility of being able to keep a loaded gun in their home for self-defense, meaning that such use of a gun does not need to explained or justified at all.

The degree to which current gun research continues to exist in an orbit totally removed and separate from public opinion and policy about the social utility of guns can best be understood by considering the report issued by the Institute of Medicine, another branch of the National Academies, setting research priorities for gun violence that had been requested by President Obama following the massacre at Sandy Hook.[22] This report made no mention of the 2005 document, nor did it attempt to evaluate whether any of the objectives of that report had been met. Rather than look at whether the data that was lacking in 2005 had been accessed or used to develop answers to questions which, according to the experts, could not be understood given gaps in the extant information, the IOM report issued nine years later set out an entirely new agenda of issues for which the lack of information made it still difficult, if not impossible, to develop a coherent and comprehensive public policy towards guns.

In brief, the IOM report listed five research priorities which needed to be addressed over the next 3-5 years. These included the characteristics of firearm violence, risks and protective factors, intervention and strategies, safe guns and the influence of video games. This is all fine and well except for the fact that all of these subjects have been studied multiple times over the last twenty years, much of it summarized by Hemenway in 2007, and the results are always the same. I can sum up this vast body of research today by quoting the words of the novelist Walter Mosley, "If you carry a gun, it's bound to go off sooner or later." And what the feds seem unable to figure out after twenty years of research with the same results again and again is that the issue gets down to this: When the gun does go off, will it have a positive or negative result?

The gun lobby and its political/media allies know the answer to that one; they have known it since 1994 and they have substantial success promoting the answer in legislation and, more important, in the attitudes that gun owners have towards the social utility of their guns. In the 1980's, before the great public arguments about guns occurred, two-thirds of all gun owners reported that they kept guns primarily for recreational shooting and hunting, aka sport. Guns as a means of self-protection came in a distant third; i.e., 33% thought that self-defense was the main reason that they owned a gun. Over the last twenty years, while public health researchers have been tirelessly working away to study the negative social impact of guns, the result of recent polls of gun owners shows that their reason for keeping a gun has exactly reversed: two-thirds now say self-defense is their chief priority; the NRA's argument has won.[23]

No wonder pro-gun researchers like Kleck and Lott don't need to re-examine and revise their own research along the lines suggested by the Academy report in 2005. What Kleck and Lott said about the positive social utility of guns has been validated by the only audience that for them really counts: the people who buy and own guns. As for those who continue to produce scholarship which demonstrates the negative social utility of guns, they still haven't figured out how to advance their arguments beyond the scholarly journals and academic conferences which showcase their work. While the number of seriously-researched articles on gun violence continues to grow, the laws controlling the ownership and use of guns continue to disappear. You would think that as a consumer item, particularly a consumer item with the potential lethality of guns became more mainstream, the degree to which it would be regulated would increase. This is what has happened, for example, with off-road vehicles like ATV's. But in the case of guns the reverse has been true—the relationship between ownership and regulation has been inverse. Which brings us to our last chapter and our last question: Can or should this relationship be made to change?

CHAPTER 6

WHY DO WE LIKE GUNS?

In 2002 the documentary film-maker Michael
Moore released a movie, *Bowling for Columbine*, which
won an Academy Award and elevated Moore to an
unquestioned position of eminence in the American
film industry. The movie opened to overwhelmingly
enthusiastic reviews, set records for documentary box
office sales both in the U.S. and abroad, and briefly
re-ignited the debate over gun control that had
languished after the Columbine High School massacre
in 1999.

One of the earliest moments in the film involved
Moore interviewing John Nichols, the brother of
Terry Nichols who, along with Timothy McVeigh,
was convicted of the Oklahoma City bombing that
destroyed the Murrah Federal Building and killed 168
people in 1995. Moore interviewed Nichols, who at
the time was an "organic farmer" raising soy-beans
for tofu, because McVeigh had stayed in his house for
several months and although Nichols was also

charged with helping build and test the explosive devices that were used in the attack, he was ultimately released for lack of evidence and went back to his organic farm.

So the interview begins with Moore talking to Nichols about his mushrooms and tofu and you're expecting this guy to be some kind of old hippie who sits at the opposite end of the political spectrum from his brother and McVeigh. But Moore is much too clever for that. After setting up the audience to expect one thing, Moore gives them something very much else, because it turns out that Nichols is a rabid gun nut and hard-core phobic who keeps a 44 magnum under his pillow because he's going to make sure that he won't be "enslaved" by the government, because if that happens, then "blood will run in the streets."

It further turns out that McVeigh and the Nichols Brothers used to attend meetings of the Michigan Militia, a bunch of whose members get some frame-time in the movie with Moore dead-panning through an interview with several of the guys while their confreres bang away at various targets with their AR-15s. Knowing that they are going to be "starring" in a Hollywood film, the Militia members all appear and sound quite rational, sober, and make a point of saying that they aren't "extremists" or "kooks," but just honest citizens who believe it's everyone's right and "duty" to defend God, country, family from…and here it gets a little vague. What exactly are the threats that the Michigan Militia and other selfsame groups are training so diligently to overcome?

For more guidance on this issue, because Michael Moore didn't seem anxious to push these folks too far, I took a look at their website, www.michiganmilitia.com, and here's what the militia says about itself:

A well-armed citizenry is the best form of Homeland Security and can better deter disasters, crime, invasion, terrorism, tyranny. Our intention is to inform, promote and facilitate the development and training of the militia. Everyone is welcome, regardless of race, creed, color, tint, or hue, religion (or a lack thereof), political affiliation (or a lack thereof), provided you do not wish to bring harm to our country or people. If you are a United States citizen (or have declared your intent to become such) who is capable of bearing arms, or supports the right to do so…then you ARE the militia.

The website appears to have been created somewhere around 2004, and its rhetoric already appears rather quaint, in particular the ethnic, religious and political inclusiveness. With all due respect to the Militia's view of itself as being the frontline of defense against all kinds of disasters— natural, military, political—there's almost a childlike lightheartedness to the innocent attempt to make sure that nobody could be insulted or offended by what they believe they will do.

But even more amusing and reflective of this seemingly genuine blamelessness is a series of descriptions of what the various specialists are expected to do as militia members, all of which is preceded by the following warning:

> THE SOUTHEAST MICHIGAN VOLUNTEER MILITIA IS ON A YELLOW ALERT, MEANING THAT WE FEEL A SITUATION IS PROBABLE. THIS IS DUE TO 9/11 LATER THIS WEEK, THREATS FROM ISIS, AND A COMPPLETELY UNSECURE BORDER. THERE ARE REPORTS THAT SOME FORM OF IMMINENT ON THE SOUTHWESTERN U.S. CHECK YOUR GEAR, FILL YOUR GAS TANKS AND WATER CONTAINERS. CONTACT YOUR TEAM LEADERS OR OTHER SMVM STAFF.

I write this section of the book on September 16, hence the reference to 9/11, which evidently came and went without any attack on the homeland to which the Michigan Militia could have responded in force. I am also not clear about the warning about loading up on gasoline because if there were to be, as they mentioned, an attack on the U.S.–Mexican border, it would take these hardy militiamen the better part of a week to drive down to the Rio Grande, by which time if there had been any type of military or terrorist incident worthy of notice they would probably find themselves in a massive traffic jam caused by all the sightseers who wanted to be able to tell their neighbors and friends that they had actually seen where the attack took place, along with the mobile taco vendors who would be hawking their munchies to the crowds.

But while I'm making light of the militia's rhetoric and bravado, I don't want to create the impression that these aren't serious folks. To begin with, you don't just join the Michigan Militia by showing up at one of their meetings or shooting sessions. You have to meet readiness requirements that were developed "after much discussion and field experimentation." And these requirements were developed so that all Militia members could defend their way of life against "terrorism, tyranny, crime, invasion, or any other threat or emergency."

The minimum requirements, or what the Militia Individual Readiness Guide refers to as Basic Readiness, requires every member to show up with a rifle, 100 rounds of ammo, a container with at least one quart of water, a cleaning kit for the rifle, suitable carrying gear, individual first-aid kit and combat or hiking boots. With all this equipment, the prospective Militia member must then complete a two-mile hike within 48 minutes, field strip and clean the weapon, and place 8 out of 20 shots into a 9-inch circle at 100 yards. And just to make sure that we can tell the good guys from the bad guys, every member must have a military-style hat with the word "militia" clearly visible, and the overall uniform should be camo, or "other uniforms as determined by tactical need, such as snow camouflage."

Before we go further into the readiness of the Michigan Militia, let's back up a bit. These paramilitary organizations with their emphasis on armed defense and patriotism mixed together with varying degrees of right-wing paranoia got their start back in the 60's and 70's with something called the *Posse Comitatus*, a militaristically modern version of the Ku Klux Klan that came out of the same racist and anti-Semitic balliwick.[1] They didn't have the internet in those days, so communication took the form of poorly-designed and badly-printed newsletters that circulated among members who were organized in local chapters with some kind of loose, confederation-style of hierarchical leadership. As an organization these militias never really amounted to anything more than an occasional public demonstrations targeting much the same "threats" as those defined by the Birchers and other right-wing, conspiracy-minded groups.

Even though a few of the really hard-core types banded together in survivalist communes in Idaho or in abandoned mining towns in Nevada and other parts of the West, with the exception of a few high-profile incidents like the standoff at Ruby Ridge, these home-grown insurrectionists or super-patriots or whatever they considered themselves never represented any real threat beyond giving a headache to the more respectable members of the community and creating an occasional bit of excitement that was usually kept under control by the local cops.[2] From time to time there would be talk about non-compliance or avoidance of tax payments and the federal government was always some kind of bogey-man intent on robbing the honest folk of their hard-won liberties and constitutional rights, but nobody ever took these groups very seriously nor did they ever constitute any real threat to the established order or the establishment of any kind.

This all changed with the bombing of the Oklahoma City Murrah Federal Building in 1995, an event which followed directly on the heels of the Clinton gun control laws that were passed in 1994. I make the connection between these events not because there was any actual connection, but rather because it was the passage of the Brady and Assault Weapons bills that sparked the NRA to begin taking a much more belligerent and loud stance in the gun debate, with the consequent sharpening of political rhetoric in which the federal government was pictured as the "enemy" of people's constitutional rights. And it was less than a week after the bombing that President Clinton made specific reference to the "extremist" rhetoric of conservative commentators like Rush Limbaugh to justify his claim that domestic terrorism was now a serious threat.

When I was a kid in the 50s, we used the term "patriot" almost exclusively to refer to men who fought and were cited for bravery in the military. In fact I was in the last group that was subject to the universal military draft; military service became a lottery in 1969 (I was drafted in 1968), and while registration continues, actual military service other than through voluntary enlistments ended in 1973.

When the militia movement began to grow after the Waco fiasco in 1993, the notion of patriotism among these hard-core extremists came to embrace not defending the country by dint of military service, but fighting against "threats" to "liberty" on the part of a national government that traditional patriots used to defend. In 2013 the Southern Poverty Legal Center identified 1,096 "anti-government 'patriot' groups," of which 240 were militias, with least one militia group in virtually every state.[3]

Most of the current-day militia organizations have websites so it's easy to float around the internet and get a quick understanding of what the groups are all about. And virtually all of them have three attributes in common: (1) Their members are all "patriots;" (2) they all defend the Constitution; and (3) they promote armed self-defense. The messages are overtly and conservatively political, there's always some reference to "tyranny" or other forms of abuse of government power, and organizational activities, which are much more social than anything remotely resembling military training, usually involve shooting and guns. Publicly these militias go out of their way to emphasize that they are law-abiding and, I'm not being sarcastic, I am sure they are. In fact, change the rhetoric somewhat, make the *raison d'etre* charity rather than self-defense, get rid of the camo clothing and meet at the local Chinese restaurant instead of the local shooting range (most militia members appear to be extremely well-fed), and the militia transmogrifies itself into the local Rotary Club with sideburns and beards.

Over the last twenty years, the traditional link between patriotism and military service has disappeared. In fact, to the extent that warfare as we practice it is increasingly a function of technology controlled by a few highly-paid volunteers, if we were to continue to link patriotism to the military there wouldn't be enough patriots to go around. And since patriotism will always find an audience or, in the case of guns a consumer, the word "patriot" has come to represent an attitude, a set of political beliefs and a life-style that revolves around guns. A perfect example is the singer Ted Nugent, whose sales of more than 40 million albums testifies to his remarkable musical talents that are displayed on the national concert tour that he leads each year. But Nugent, who never served in the armed forces, describes himself as a "patriot" and makes headlines on a frequent basis by dint of extremely provocative, anti-liberal rants. Here's one of them that he let loose just prior to the 9/11 anniversary in 2014:

> 9-11-14 is the day of infamy again. Unarmed & helpless Americans and

Europeans will be viciously ambushed when they least expect it, and the death toll will be more brutal and widespread than all the peace & love dreamers could ever imagine. Those who carry guns had better gun & ammo up no matter where you go, carrying at least 10 spare mags or 10 spare speedloaders because the allahpukes are confident they will once again methodically slaughter walking cowering whining cryin helpless sitting ducks capable of zero resistance. To gullible naive embarrassing ill prepared targets, there is still time to firepower up ASAP. Head for cover but retain an attentiveness in order to identify the evildoers and dbl tap center mass, then two to the head. Then take cover and prepare your next evasive escape, taking dwn known jihadists to the best of your ability, Aim small miss small center mass & headshots, This is going to be the real deal & absolutely survivable against these 4th world allahpuke zombies. STAND! Go heavy, Only assholes are outgunned, Dont be outgunned or out ammo'd. Goodluck. Be safe, Shoot straight & OFTEN, Godspeed, killemall[4]

Note the frequent references to guns and being prepared to use arms for defense against terrorist attacks. As far as I know, Nugent himself has never been involved in any kind of armed fracas, but from tidbits like "double tap center mass" and "take cover and prepare your next evasive escape," you would think he had just gone through a no-holds-barred firefight with the enemy all shot up and left for dead. No doubt Nugent's rants in this respect are somewhat self-serving from a marketing point of view, because, among other side hustles, he puts his name and face on an ammunition line which hasn't yet threatened Winchester or Remington for shelf space but you never know. On the other hand, what's really behind this rhetoric is the recognition on Nugent's part that connecting guns to patriotism and patriotism to armed self-defense strikes a chord with many people who own guns, particularly if, like the members of these militia groups, they build their social activities and life-styles around playing with their guns.

That's right. I consciously used the phrase "playing with guns" because that's what these folks do. When I was a kid we played "Cowboys and Indians" with our guns because it was in the cowboy movies that we saw guns being used. And in all of these games, nobody ever took the on the role of an Indian; we could "see" the Indians and "shoot" at the Indians but of course they really didn't exist. In reality, all those terrorists that the militias are protecting us against don't exist either. Yes, they flew planes into the World Trade Center, the Pentagon and into the ground near Shanksville, PA. And yes, they have blown up hotels in India, American diplomatic stations in Libya and commuter trains in Spain. And yes, they are forcing us back into a ground war in the Near East. All of those events really happened, all cost lives, and all of them in some way or another represent some kind of threat. But none of these militia groups will ever do anything more to defend America than we did as kids by going into the park and pretending that our toy guns were Winchester repeating rifles which killed all the Red Men who came riding over the bluff. There was no bluff, there were no Red Men, but it was a lot of fun.

However, the problem is that because these militia folks have real guns, the line between fantasy and reality starts to get a little blurred. Not that ISIS is going to invade Fowlerville, Michigan, or any of the other small towns in Livingston County where the Michigan Militia claims to have a base. But the fact that there's an enemy out there—somewhere—who poses some kind of threat to something, and the fact that I have a real gun that I can use to protect myself and others from that threat, means that our ability to dress up as if we were in the armed services and shoot a gun as if we were in the armed forces allows us as adults to feel that the game we are now playing is for real. And the fact that the gun shoots live ammo is very important, because this is something that these game-players never could do in the military because there was and is no military in which they can serve.

Recall that the NRA and hard-core gun nuts first made their presence felt in the debate that led to the passage of the Brady bill and the Assault Weapons ban in 1994. This was the same year that the first Americans came of age who were not subject to the draft. And the good news about serving in the military is that until the Vietnam War made it unsustainable, the draft was universal and just about all able-bodied men had to serve. Which meant that just about all able-bodied men in America learned how to use a gun. And what was the purpose of learning how to shoot the M-16 and the 1911 Colt? It was to protect us against our enemies, and in this man's army, the enemies were real. And in this man's army you didn't have to pretend that there was a "bad guy" out there waiting to shoot you if you didn't get him first; you had those nasty sergeants walking up and down the firing line kicking you in the butt if you didn't put 5 rounds inside that zero every time you picked up your gun. From his rhetoric you'd never guess that Ted Nugent isn't a veteran, but he's not. He's just another grown-up playing the 21st century version of cowboys and Indians with his trusty AR-15 instead of a Winchester 94.

For the men of my generation and the generation that came before me, military service was a *rite de passage,* and even though it was usually far less then it was cracked up to be, it was something that just about every male experienced who was born between 1920 and 1950, and when you were finished doing your duty you went home knowing all there was to know about how to protect yourself and others with a gun. Which is why neither my father or any of his war buddies ever kept a gun around their homes. They weren't farmers, they weren't hunters, they lived in houses which often didn't even have locks on the doors. My parents moved into a residential neighborhood in New York City in 1956 and my father finally got around to installing a lock on the front door when he put the house up for sale in 1968.

The watershed that changed this situation were the gun bills that Clinton got through Congress in 1994. Because by that time there was (or at least there was the perception of) a major spike in crime, there was a vociferous and politicized NRA, and, most important, there was a generation coming of age who had no real-time experience in using guns. Looking back over the last twenty years, I have to admit that from a marketing point of view, the NRA's decision to politicize its message by demonizing gun-grabbing liberals and justifying gun ownership as the first and most important line of personal defense can only be considered a master stroke. Because not only did their argument give gun owners a patriotic rationale for owning their guns, but it also created a threat to this ownership, an "enemy" of gun ownership which could be resisted without having to serve in the real armed forces at all.

But the marketing skill and insight of the NRA went far beyond creating a political bogey-man that could be a target for the anger if gun owners who felt that their guns might be taken away. What they really understood and began shaping their message to embrace was the idea that for most American men, military service was a *rite de passage* that could be replicated and re-invented to a certain extent by ready access and use of guns. In the neighborhood where I grew up every single male served in a branch of the armed forces and it was expected that every male of my generation would do the same. And while military service started to be disparaged during the Vietnam conflict, the anti-war sentiment was a product largely of college campuses, while for the rest of the country, and certainly a majority of its draft-age men, taking a stance against the military was for kooks, fags, college boys and so forth, and for everyone else service in the armed forces was just something you had to do.

Many of the guys who joined militia and paramilitary groups in the 1990's were guys for whom military service had passed them by. But what had *not* passed them by, and this was certainly also true for those of us who were drafted into active duty, was membership in another paramilitary organization, complete with uniforms, devotion to duty, country and firearms training known as the Boy Scouts of America. Originally founded in England in 1910 by Robert Baden-Powell, the scouting movement drew its basic inspiration from a book written by Baden-Powell, *Scouting For Boys*, which was a watered-down version of a military manual that Baden-Powell wrote and used to train British troops during the Boer War. The scouting movement drew heavily on the notions of preparedness, initiative, self-reliance, loyalty, patriotism and discipline, with the basic theme being that such traits would engender a healthy, well-developed and morally righteous leadership class.

The scouting movement spread rapidly throughout the British Commonwealth and the United States, with American chapters springing up almost as quickly as they were appearing in England. Scouting emphasized a combination of sportsmanship, patriotism and character-building through achieving goals defined by the merit badge system, of which one of the earliest badges was for marksmanship. Many scouting units, including the one to which I belonged, were given World War I surplus training rifles that had been chambered in 22LR in order to save on the costs of ammunition. Most scout campgrounds had a rifle range where kids could sharpen their shooting skills.

I don't think there was a single small or medium-sized town in America which didn't have a well-organized scout group that included young kids in cub scout packs, middle teen boys in scout troops, older boys in the Explorer program and girl scouts who started off in the Brownie program beginning at age six or seven through nine. Even though numbers have dropped off a bit in the last several decades, girl scouts remain one of America's favorite charitable activities largely because their cookies, sold since 1917, go into American homes at the rate of several hundred million every year.

So we have a long tradition of civilians learning as kids to walk around in uniforms and learning how to shoot guns. But we shouldn't try to push this argument too far in terms of connecting the Boy Scouts to today's argument about guns for the simple reason that the appeal to patriotism that underlay scouting culture was an unblemished appeal to "my country right or wrong," so to speak, whereas the patriotism of the militia movement and the utilization of guns to enhance and sustain patriotic values defines "my country" in certain, politically-partisan ways, a definition that has been adopted and now strongly promoted by the NRA.

The NRA may claim, as it does, that among its membership Republicans outnumber Democrats by a margin of two to one, but the only registered member of the Democratic Party that I ever encountered at the NRA meeting was—me. Whenever the NRA convention falls on the year of a Presidential election, you can be sure that many, if not all of the putative Republican candidates show up to press the flesh and exhort the crowd. But I have never seen a single elected or electable official from the Democratic Party at the NRA meeting, and it goes without saying that NRA mail and email lists are the stock in trade of virtually every Republican fundraising effort that is mounted before, during and after political campaigns.

The fact that the Republican Party has, since the election of Obama, pictured itself not only as the defender of the homeland from terrorism both here and abroad but has also become the defender of the Constitution against attempts to usurp it or secretly change it by those Socialist-inspired *apparatchiks* on the Left, dovetails neatly into the NRA's promotion of gun ownership as a means not only of self-defense but of maintaining American preparedness against threats to our freedom both from here and from abroad. In this respect, gun ownership is not so much an active way to make America a safer place, but rather a symbol of what we all want America to be.

But who is this "we?" Well, it used to be fifty-year old white men who lived in small towns, had trouble getting through high school and drove a truck. And in many parts of the country this is still a significant demographic, but it's on the way out. And even the Republicans know that relying on this voter base to maintain parity as a national party just isn't going to work, in the same way that the NRA knows that this demographic won't sustain gun sales too far ahead. So while the NRA continues to champion itself as America's first and foremost collection of patriots, it also is looking to move guns towards acceptance by other consumer demographics for whom the patriotism argument just doesn't really wash, and this means getting guns into the mainstream by selling them to people who just want to have fun.

This is why the industry tries with such vehemence to promote the sale of assault-style rifles and small, concealable pistols; not so much because there's any truth to the idea that owning one of these items will make you or your family safer from crime, terrorists or anything else. Rather, because these are the guns that everyone sees in movies, videos and TV. The ultimate vindication of the gun industry will not happen because they can convince everyone that guns will make us more safe; it will come when average consumers look at guns the way they look at droids or iPhones; it's not so much that they are actually indispensable, rather, they serve some kind of vaguely-defined "need" and, more important, let you pick it up, play with it, put it down. The average American smartphone user has downloaded 32 apps; the average AR-15 owner usually keeps at least 500 .223 cartridges around.

And this is the great challenge that the gun industry faces: how do you get rid of the notion that guns are violent and replace it with the idea that guns are fun? For one thing, you design them not for a specific need like hunting, but just for shooting, and not shooting in a competitive sense, but just shooting for fun. It used to be that the only people who went to shooting ranges were the hardcore gun competitors who were serious hobbyists, which meant they spent all their time messing around with their guns: tuning them, modifying them, working on them; picture those young men who used to spend all weekend bending into the open hoods of their cars. They also went to shooting matches, sometimes spending serious money to travel to Camp Perry in Ohio to compete against other gunnies from all over the place.

The gun hobbyist culture continues to exist, of course, but alongside it has emerged the idea of shooting by the amateurs who just want to pull the trigger of a live gun because it's fun. This type of shooting activity, often conducted with automatic weapons, has replaced the old, county fair shooting gallery of days gone by, and if it weren't for some unfortunate events such as an occasional child shooting themselves to death, I suspect that this type of activity would spread rapidly in entertainment resorts like Orlando and other places where families go to have fun.

The whole point of the NRA and gun maker strategy is to use both the arguments from fear and the arguments from entertainment to promote the acceptance of guns. The only problem, however, is that try as they might, no matter what the rationale gun sales continue to be spurred primarily by a concern among current gun owners that they might lose their toys. And where gun ownership is the norm, like the South, the rural Midwest and the mountain states in the West, appeals to protecting guns no matter what the reason tend to bear fruit. Where gun ownership is the exception and not the rule, on the other hand, more, not less gun controls become the order of the day. In the year following Sandy Hook, more than 1,500 bills that both tightened or loosened gun controls were introduced in state legislatures all over the country.[5] Of these measures, 109 became laws, of which 39 created more controls and 70 made it easier either to own, buy or carry guns. Of the 39 more restrictive laws that were enacted, only 9 were passed in states where the GOP had control of both the legislature and the governor's mansion, whereas 25 came out of blue states and 5 were from states where political control was mixed. On the other hand, 49 of the 70 new laws that loosened gun controls came out of red states, 18 came from states with mixed, blue-red control and only 3 were enacted in states which had blue majorities in the legislature and a Democratic governor signing the final bill.

If you live in one of 14 states that consider gun ownership to be of concern (by that I mean there is some degree of state government intervention in the buying and selling of guns), you are one of roughly 115 million people whose access to firearms is beyond your own control. The remaining 200 million Americans live in states where gun ownership is still basically defined by a combination of the Gun Control Act of 1968 and the Brady Bill of 1994. And while many of the states that go beyond GCA-Brady have tried in one way or another to make gun ownership an issue of serious, legislative concern, the fact is that even in places with the strictest controls, such as New York City, it doesn't take much initiative or energy to get your hands on a gun. When I lived in New York City I used to go up to a gun show in Kingston, New York, about an hour's drive north of Manhattan, with a couple of off-duty New York City cops, one of whom had been a college classmate of mine and the other who was the head of the borough's SWAT team in his spare time. I say in his "spare time" because he spent most of his time on the job building up a very impressive dossier of x-rays and other medical evidence which he eventually used to retire with a disability pension due to some so-called problem with his knees, money which he then used to support a bagel, coffee and lottery kiosk at one of the local malls.

Every three months or so there was a gun show at the armory in Kingston and we would drive up with a bundle of cash. It would usually take about ten minutes for all of us to spot the treasures we wanted to take home, which were then purchased "on shield," as the saying went, with no questions asked. In Chapter 3 I relate how I briefly owned a beautiful Smith & Wesson Model 58 in 41 magnum that I picked up at a gun show and almost immediately traded it for some newfangled thing called a Glock. At another show I remember scoffing up without any concern about paperwork a mint Walther P-38 that had been manufactured just prior to World War II. Yeah, yeah, I know how the ATF has cracked down on gun shows, but two years ago when my wife and I walked through a show in Lebanon, Pennsylvania, in the time it took Carolyn to buy a couple of sets of earrings and bracelets, I handed over some cash, no questions asked, for a 3-inch S&W Model 36.

Which brings me to the end of this book and to the end of the four books that I have written about guns. So perhaps it's time to sum things up. What follows is a brief list of what I consider the real gun issues to be. What I mean by real issues are the ideas and notions about guns on both sides which continue to drive the argument. And then I'll conclude with what I think needs to be done to settle the argument once and for all.

1. **America has the highest rate of gun violence of any advanced (OECD) country**. If we define gun violence as the deaths and injuries that are caused by guns; i.e., mortality and morbidity, the statement from a statistical point of view is true. From the point of view of public policy it's a meaningless statement because we are the only OECD country in which the overwhelming bulk

of gun violence is experienced by two very distinct populations (inner-city, minority males ages 16-26 for homicide and assault, white males in small towns and smaller cities particularly in the West), who if we lift these two demographics out of the overall mortality and morbidity counts, our gun violence rate is high but not exceedingly higher than the rest of the OECD.

2. **Allowing for every measurable economic and social factor, our elevated rate of gun violence is a function of the existence of so many civilian-owned guns**. Statistically true, but it can be looked at in a much different way. The overall gun homicide rate for the OECD (not including the U.S.) is between .05 and 2 homicides per 100,000 population. The average per capita gun ownership ranged between 0.5 and 30 per 100 persons. Our numbers are 5 and 90 respectively. But if you were to adjust all the other per capita ownership rates to our rate and then adjust the gun homicide rate accordingly, the rest of the OECD would have gun homicide rates between 2 and 5 times higher than our rate. And this makes us so violent?

3. **Expanding background checks to cover all gun transfers would substantially reduce the number of guns that get into the "wrong" hands.** According to the ATF, roughly 200,000 guns were reported missing or stolen in 2012.[6]

This is the *reported* number; the real number must be higher. Let's say that two-thirds of these guns are old junkers which no self-respecting criminal would ever want to use. That still leaves over 80,000 guns that head for the street each year, and this doesn't include the guns whose disappearance isn't noticed, isn't reported, or both. If one-third of all American households contain firearms, this means that somewhere around 80 to 90 million American adults own guns that could wind up being stolen or otherwise out in the street. And if one-tenth of one percent of all these guns represents the arsenal that might wind up in the wrong hands each year, then how many "irresponsible" gun owners does this represent? In the overall scheme of things: not many.

4. **The only thing that stops a bad guy with a gun is a good guy with a gun**. The FBI conducted a study of 160 "active" shootings that occurred between 2000 and 2013, defining an active shooting as an incident where multiple victims were shot and in which "both law enforcement personnel *and citizens* [my italics] have the potential to affect the outcome of the event based upon their response." These multiple shootings resulted in 1,043 persons getting killed, and this number did not include the shooter who in some cases also turned the gun on himself.

How many times were such incidents affected in any way by a citizen using a gun? Once.

5. **Violent crime rates go down as the number of armed citizens goes up.** There has been a 50% reduction in violent crime over the past twenty years, the same period during which concealed-carry permits are now issued more or less routinely in just about all 50 states. Of course the fact that someone has a CCW permit in his wallet doesn't mean that he's got a gun in his pocket and there has never been a single study which gives any numbers on the percentage of CCW-holders who actually walk around carrying a gun. But leaving that hole in the data aside, the fact is that violent crime in general and gun violence in particular has experienced its steepest decline in the jurisdiction which remains populated by an overwhelmingly unarmed citizenry; i.e. New York City, which still operates under the 1910 Sullivan Law which effectively prevents just about anyone from carrying a gun, yet gun crime in New York has decreased by more than 80 percent in the past twenty years.

As for the gun argument, we seem to be a country that argues very loudly about very insignificant issues and events. This year, for example, more than 5 million Americans will die because of their addiction to smoking, a disease which keeps less than 12,000 people in business growing tobacco on their farms. What would it cost us to give each of these farmers a couple of million dollars to shut down their farms? Believe me it's a small fraction of what we pay each year for the medical and social costs of dealing with the use of what they grow. And cashing these farmers off their land would be a one-time charge. The CDC estimates that the number of smoking deaths by 2030 will climb to more than 7 million.

We made a decision in the 1980's to keep these farmers in business but to regulate the sale of their product by keeping cigarettes out of the "wrong hands," in this case, hands belonging to kids. Sound familiar? Keeping something out of the wrong hands? Know what it would cost to shut down the commercial production of handguns except for some tightly-controlled civilian sales, as well as supplying the military and the police? Probably about the same as it would cost to move those tobacco farmers off their land. Do you really believe that the same country that couldn't shut down tobacco farming and save five million lives a year is going to shut down an industry whose products result in only 30,000 deaths? I'm sorry if my concerns about gun mortality and morbidity sound a little caustic and unconcerned. But I have a sneaking suspicion that the real reason the argument about guns is so loud and yet so inconclusive is because nobody really cares whether guns are a problem or not.

Want my solution to the gun violence problem? I'll end this book the way I end all my books, by relating a little anecdote, and I'll leave it to the reader to figure out what it means. From 1985 to 1990 I had a little side hustle in New York City importing guns from the Caribbean and shipping them to a friendly gun nut in Arizona named Joe DeSaye. Joe owned a wholesale business called J&G, which was named after himself and his wife Grace, even though they were divorced. Joe's stock in trade was used guns which he would buy in large batches and then sell mail-order to dealers nationwide. He ran an eight-page ad in a wholesale sheet called *Shotgun News*, a current copy of which could always be found in the guard room of the Criminal Courts building on Centre Street in lower Manhattan.

Joe and I had done business over the years and we liked and trusted each other often to the tune of hundreds of thousands of dollars in cold cash. So one day Joe calls me in New York and tells me that he's got it from the "inside" that the Postal Inspectors were going to be buying new guns and that every Inspector, some 4,000 of them, had turned in their old guns which were now sitting in a warehouse at the FBI training center in Quantico, VA, just outside of

Washington, D.C. And Joe further knew that the guns were in immaculate shape and that they were all kinds of makes and models because the Inspectors had been allowed to carry whatever type of handgun they could. And finally, Joe knew something else, namely, that nobody else knew about these guns and that someone pretty high up in the Postal Service was willing to sell them to Joe. Which meant selling them to me and Joe because any really big deal was a deal swung between him and me.

So a couple of days later I'm being waved through the gate at Quantico and after stopping at an inner gate to be verified, I'm now driving behind one of those innocuous Chevrolet coupes which the FBI uses because they believe nobody can tell it's them. We pull up in front of a warehouse, one of these corrugated steel buildings with no windows and one door; the agent unlocks a single lock, I step inside, he turns on the lights and I am transformed in one second into someone from another place in time.

Do you have any idea what 4,000 guns look like piled in 20 neat piles, each pile counting 250 guns? Do you have any idea what it's like to pick up a perfect, originally-blued Colt Single Action Army revolver in 44 that was probably manufactured around 1910? Do you have any idea what it's like to hold ten of them? And then pick up a Smith &

Wesson Model 52 auto pistol chambered for 38 special wadcutter, possibly the most accurate factory-tuned gun ever made? And then put it down and pick up four more? Can you imagine how my heart sang when I walked over to not one but two piles of Colt 1911 Commercial models with the royal blue finish that were made (because they had the date of production on the slides) between 1919 and 1923?

Actually, you can't imagine it. Because I can't really describe in words the feeling of absolute rapture as I walked around that room. And the real problem I had at that moment was to figure out how to tell Joe DeSaye that I wanted to keep at least 500 of the guns. That's the problem with the gun business. You're in the gun business because you really love the things, and it doesn't matter whether you make a living or not because you can't explain to anyone who isn't a gun nut why you can't ever stop wanting to own guns.

So here's my solution to gun violence. And I really mean what I'm going to say. I think that people who enjoy hunting should be able to own all the guns that they want to on as long as they are really guns that one would use on a hunt. And with all due respect to the stupid and self-serving nonsense peddled by the NSSF, I'm sorry but an assault rifle is simply not a "modern sporting rifle" no matter what they say. It's an assault rifle plain and simple, an adult toy that lets people think they are defending the homeland when all they are doing is shooting off a lot of 223, and as far as I'm concerned they could all be sent over to be used by the Taliban, ISIS, or whatever freedom-fighting band the CIA wants to arm next.

As for handguns, if it's so important to keep a gun or guns in the house for self-defense then you should be willing to register the gun so that the police can be immediately notified if it's stolen or just thrown away. The NRA opposes registration because it will lead to guns being taken away—that's pure crap and they know it. The NRA is opposed to registration because it knows that the moment you have to register your guns, then gun sales will sharply decline. And the idea that an "armed" citizenry is a "free" citizenry belongs in the same wastebasket of ideas where I'd like to throw every prediction that schmucky Dick Morris ever made about how ruinous inflation would erupt before the end of Obama's first term.

But what about all the gun nuts, people like me? It' very simple; if you want to have a lot of handguns lying around because you love them so much, you spend 30 bucks and get a federal collector's license, known as a C&R, and keep an accurate log of all your guns. You might get inspected once in your lifetime by the ATF, but just having your guns under some kind of license which requires that you keep a record of their existence would be enough in 99% of all cases to make sure that the guns would stay where they belong. I don't think it's too much to ask people like me who can't live without their guns to pony up a thirty-dollar license fee every three years.

Incidentally, the deal for the Postal Inspector's guns fell through. Want to know why? Because just around the time I was going to submit the bid, and I was the only person bidding on the guns, some dope in some Southern town shot someone and it turned out that the gun he used had been sold by the police department to a local dealer who then resold it to a customer who then gave it to his brother-in-law, you know the drill. And the problem was that the gun had the name of the police department etched into the backstrap or the frame, so everyone was walking around saying how that particular department had sold the "killer gun."

Well it turned out that every last one of those Postal Inspector guns had the initials "USPS" etched onto the barrel or the slide or the frame of each gun. And somewhere high up in the postal system brass got cold feet because as much as they wanted the money for all that used steel, they were simply scared that some asshole would shoot some other asshole with one of those guns and they would be accused of letting the damn things get out into the street. I even flew back down to D.C. and told them that we would roll over the letters before re-selling any of the guns but it was an argument I couldn't win. Several months later I found out that the guns had all been crated up, loaded on a C-130 transport at Andrews and (this truly breaks my heart) dumped out at sea. That's right—my beautiful Colts and Smiths were pushed out of the back of an airplane never to be seen or touched again.

And that's how I really feel about guns and that's what I think America ought to do with its guns. Either find a way for the people who love guns to buy them, keep them, trade them or sell them (notice I didn't say shoot them), or get rid of them. Dump them out at sea. Because there's no other way to keep guns out of the "wrong" hands. Which wouldn't be the worst thing in the world; i.e., if we didn't keep guns out of the "wrong" hands. After all, smoking kills a lot more people than guns and we know that cigarettes get into the wrong hands every time that someone walks into the mini-mart and buys a pack. If we're willing to let people continue to kill themselves with cigarettes, why not with guns?

Here's a recent email that I received from a company selling what they call the Field Survivor Tool.

Field Survivor Tool

Imagine having every tool you need to get your AR back in service right from your pistol grip. The Samson Field Survivor is a multi-tool system that stores inside the AR Magpul Miad and MOE pistol grip. (NOTE: Magpul grip is not included with tool.)

- Broken shell extractor
- Wire brush for bore cleaning
- Ampule for oil for one field lube
- Cable to pull the brush through the bore
- Carbon cleaning tool
- Flat blade screwdriver
- Feed lip adjustment tool
- Gas key cleaning tool
- Cotter pin hook
- Strike Plate
- Front sight adjustment tool.
- Magazine feed lip gauge

The Field Survivor tool is the one tool necessary for every AR to keep you safe in Combat or in play on the range.

Notice that the tool, which retails for $79.95, will keep me safe in combat or in play at the range. No matter how many hard-core gunnies tell me that they won't let Obama or the government take away their constitutional right to defend themselves or anyone else, the fact is that none of them will ever actually have a real reason to use that that tool or the gun on which it fits. Maybe the way those toys work has changed, but the gun as a toy remains the same. If you're an adult you really can't take the Michigan Militia seriously, you know that Nugent's tantrum only works if you're very uneducated or remarkably dumb. These are adults who have found a way to continue living through the fantasies of their childhood and who am I or anyone else to say that this kind of self-made entertainment shouldn't be allowed to exist? So 30,000 die each year and another 50,000 or so wind up wounded from guns? Think about those numbers the next time you line up behind that guy who's buying a carton of cigarettes and will probably be one of those 5 or 6 million who winds up being counted as dead from cancer by the CDC. You'll get pissed off if he holds you up on the line while he ponders which lottery ticket to buy for an extra ten bucks, but you won't get scared, nervous or even concerned if it turns out what he had in his pocket was a pack of cigarettes instead of a gun.

NOTES

CHAPTER 1

1.   http://washington.everytown.org/?source=prno_wainvesti
gation&utm_source=pr_n_&utm_medium=_o&utm_campaign
=wainvestigation

2.   I wish to thank Stephen Halbrook, the NRA Counsel, for
providing me with a copy of Kleck's deposition.

3.   P. Cook, "The Great American Gun War: Four Decades in
the Trenches," University of Chicago Press, 2013, p. 21.

4.   http://www.statista.com/statistics/248845/number-of-
victims-of-mass-shootings-in-western-democratic-countries/

5.   http://webappa.cdc.gov/cgi-bin/broker.exe

6.   http://www.surgeongeneral.gov/library/reports/

7.   http://www.npr.org/2014/04/26/306837618/justice-
stevens-six-little-ways-to-change-the-constitution

8.   http://www.fbi.gov/about-us/cjis/ucr/crime-in-the-
u.s/2012/crime-in-the-u.s.-2012/offenses-known-to-law-
enforcement/expanded-homicide/expanded_homicide_data_tab
le_3_murder_offenders_by_age_sex_and_race_2012.xls

9.   http://science.howstuffworks.com/life/men-more-
violent.htm

10.   http://www.bjs.gov/content/pub/pdf/wo.pdf

11.   http://web.archive.org/web/20130703020459/http://ww
w.nrahq.org/history.asp

12.   http://bklyn-genealogy-info.stevemorse.org/Society/Cree
dmoor.html

13.   http://www.bjs.gov/content/pub/pdf/GUIC.PDF.   This
report, published by Bureau of Justice Statistics in 1995 stated

that 250,000 automatic guns had been registered with the ATF, a number which has grown to slightly under 500,000 in the most recent ATF report: http://hamptonroads.com/2012/10/virginia-tops-us-machine-gun-owners

14. http://www.dailykos.com/story/2012/12/17/1171047/-There-are-240-000-fully-automatic-guns-in-the-US-and-only-2-deaths-in-80-years

15. http://boldprogressives.org/2013/01/for-most-of-its-history-the-nra-actually-backed-sensible-gun-regulation/

16. http://supreme.justia.com/cases/federal/us/521/898/case.html

17. http://www.nytimes.com/2009/05/09/opinion/09sat4.html?_r=0

18. http://www.nytimes.com/2005/10/21/politics/21guns.html

19. http://www.ucdmc.ucdavis.edu/vprp/publications/Wintemute%20Characteristics%20of%20FFLs%20final%20proofs.pdf

20. https://ecf.dcd.uscourts.gov/cgi-bin/show_public_doc?2008cv1289-83, page 30.

21. Ibid.

22. I didn't understand the limits of so many of the research models used by gun researchers until I read, David Grimes & Kenneth Schultz, "Bias and causal associations in observational research," *The Lancet*, Vol. 359 (January 19, 2002) pp. 248-252. I only wish that more of the "experts" on gun violence would read this article. Most of them haven't.

23. Cf. Albert O. Hirschmann, *The Rhetoric of Reaction, Perversity, Futility, Jeopardy* (Cambridge, 1991). In Chapter 6 Hirschmann creates a similar typology for analyzing progressive ideas. I have used both of his models. I re-read Hirschmann's brilliant book because of a reference to it in Kristin Goss, *Disarmed, The Missing*

Movement for Gun Control in America (Princeton, 2006), p. 113 et. seq. Much of this chapter re-states, in a less-polite tone, ideas found in Philip Cook & Kristin Goss, *The Gun Debate, What Everyone Needs To Know* (Oxford, 2014.)

Chapter 2

1.   Gary Kleck, Point Blank, Guns and Violence in America (New York, 1991) p. 49.

2.   http://www.nssf.org/retailers/PDF/2014_ATFcommerce StatReport.pdf

3.   http://www.census.gov/prod/2002pubs/censr-4.pdf

4.   http://smartgunlaws.org/gun-design-safety-standards-policy-summary/. The Law center To Prevent Gun Violence advocates safer gun design on their website as an antidote to low-quality "Saturday Night Special" guns. They have no idea what cheap guns looked like before the 1968 GCA.

5.   https://www.census.gov/hhes/www/housing/housing_pa tterns/pdftoc.html

6.   Gary Kleck & Marc Gertz, "Armed Resistance To Crime: The Prevalence and Nature of Self-Defense With a Gun," Journal of Criminal Law and Criminology, Vol. 86, 1 (1995), pp. 150-86.

7.   http://www.bjs.gov/index.cfm?ty=dcdetail&iid=245#Coll ection_period

8.   You would think this would be the case since non-reporting of violent crimes ranges between 30 and 60 percent based on type of crime; the exception being homicide since it's pretty difficult to hide a body. But in fact, CDC gun mortality numbers tend to exceed the FBI numbers by 15% or more per year.

9. http://www.ndsu.edu/pubweb/~rcollins/scholarship/guns.html

10. http://www.gun-nuttery.com/rtc.php

11. http://www.cato.org/guns-and-self-defense

12. Kleck & Gertz, p. 160.

13. ibid., p. 151.

14. This is what Philip Cook referenced (Fn 2, Chap. 1) in discussing how the NRA has defined the gun issue.

15. http://www.bjs.gov/index.cfm?ty=pbdetail&iid=5113

16. Kleck & Gertz, pp. 155-56.

17. ibid., p. 156.

18. http://www.bjs.gov/content/pub/pdf/cvius94.pdf

19. Kleck & Gertz, p. 156.

20. ibid., p. 160.

21. Ibid., p. 185.

22. D. Hemenway, "The Myth of Millions of Annual Self-Defense Gun Uses: A Case Study of Survey Estimates of Rare Events," Chance (Vol. 10, 3) 1997, p. 7 et . seq.

23. http://www.bloomberg.com/news/2012-12-21/shootings-costing-u-s-174-billion-show-burden-of-gun-violence.html.

24. D. Anderson, "The Aggregate Burden of Crime," http://papers.ssrn.com/sol3/papers.cfm?abstract_id=147911, p. 30.

25. G. Kleck and M. DeLone, "Victim Resistance and Offender Weapon Effects in Robbery," Journal of Quantitative Criminology, Vol. 9, 1 (1993), pp. 55-81.

26. ibid., p. 75.

27. ibid. Needless to say, this paper was not cited by Kleck in his DGU study.

28.   http://www.foxnews.com/us/2014/01/03/detroit-police-chief-james-craig-says-more-citizens-should-be-armed/

29.   M. Wolfgang, "A Tribute To A View I Have Opposed," Journal of Criminal Law and Criminology, Vol. 86, 1 (1995), 188-92.

30.   See a detailed discussion of the Academy's findings in Chapter 5.

31.   "Draft Final Technical Report: The Impact of Victim Self protection on Rape Completion and Injury," Department of Justice, Doc. No. 211201.

32.   http://wsfrprograms.fws.gov/Subpages/LicenseInfo/HuntingLicCertHistory20042013.pdf

33.   http://www.statisticbrain.com/hunting-statistics/

34.   I deal with this issue in detail in Chapter 3.

35.   http://www.gao.gov/assets/600/592552.pdf

36.   Daniel Webster, et. al., "How Delinquent Youths Acquire Guns: Initial Versus Most Recent Gun Acquisitions," Journal of Urban Health, Vol. 79, No. 1 (March, 2002), pp. 60-69; Patrick Carter, et. al., "Firearm Possession Among Adolescents Presenting in an Urban Emergency Department for Assult," Pediatrics, Vol. 132, No. 2 (August, 2013), pp. 1-9. And the must-read article on this subject, Alan Lizotte, et. al., "Factors Influencing Gun Carrying Among Urban Males Over The Adolescent-Young Adult Life Course," Criminology, Vol. 38, No. 3 (2000), pp. 811-34.

37.   Cf., Dan Baum, Gun Guys, A Road Trip (New York, 2013). An honest and clever book about the trials and travails of someone who finally gets a concealed-carry permit and discovers that it's just too much trouble to walk around with a gun.

Chapter 3

1.   Adam Winkler, *Gunfight, The Battle Over The Right To Bear Arms In America* (New York, 2011). More than just a legal perspective, it's a well-done history of 2nd Amendment jurisprudence.

2.   I rarely use Wikipedia as a source, but the article on the growth of concealed-carry permits is exceptional and deserves to be cited and read. I used it for the data which comprises the graph. Although he and I don't agree on anything, I should also cite Brian A. Patrick, *Rise Of The Anti-Media, In-Forming America's Concealed Weapons Carry Movement* (Ohio, 2013.)

3.   http://www.people-press.org/2013/03/12/section-3-gun-ownership-trends-and-demographics/

4.   John R. Lott, Jr., *More Guns Less Crime, Understanding Crime and Gun Control Laws* (Chicago, 2010). I am using the 3rd edition.

5.   *Ibid.,* p. 20.

6.   http://www2.ed.gov/policy/elsec/leg/esea02/pg54.html

7.   http://mediamatters.org/research/2013/03/12/the-nine-worst-claims-about-guns-from-john-lott/193014.

8.   http://thomas.loc.gov/cgi-bin/query/F?r105:4:./temp/~r 10559IInw:e237884:

9.   http://mediamatters.org/research/2012/12/17/who-is-gun-advocate-john-lott/191885

10.   *More Gun, Less Crime*, op.cit., p. 63.

11.   *Ibid.,* p. 6.

12.   http://thomas.loc.gov/cgi-bin/query/F?r105:4:./temp/~r 10559IInw:e237884:

13.   Lott, *ibid.*

14.   Ian Ayres and John Donohue, "Shooting Down The 'More Guns Less Crime' Hypothesis," Stanford Law Review, Vol. 51, No. 4 (2003), pp. 1271-72.

15.   *Ibid.,* p. 1281.

16.   *Ibid.,* p. 1286.

Chapter 4

1.   http://www.nssf.org/retailers/PDF/2014_ATFcommerce StatReport.pdf

2.   Kleck, *Point Blank,* p. 49.

3.   http://usliberals.about.com/od/Election2012Factors/a/Gun-Owners-As-Percentage-Of-Each-States-Population.htm

4.   http://www.fbi.gov/about-us/cjis/ucr/crime-in-the-u.s/2012/crime-in-the-u.s.-2012/tables/20tabledatadecpdf. UCR detailed reports on crimes by type of weapon.

5.   http://www.bjs.gov/content/pub/press/fshbopc0510pr.cfm

6.   http://www.tracetheguns.org/

7.   http://www.washingtonpost.com/wp-srv/special/nation/guns/

8.   https://www.atf.gov/statistics/index.html

9.   http://www.nssc1.org/important-school-violence-statistics.html

10.   Citation in fn. 36, Chapter 2.

11.   Philip J. Cook, et. al., "Underground Gun Markets," The Economic Journal, 117 (November, 2007), pps. F588-F618.

12.   D. Hemenway & E. Richardson, "Homicide, suicide and unintentional firearm fatality: comparing the United States with other high-income countries, 2003." *Journal of Trauma.* 70, pp. 238-43.

13. D. Hemenway, "Risks and benefits of a gun in the home." *American Journal of Lifestyle Medicine.* 5(6), pp. 502-511.

14. http://webappa.cdc.gov/cgi-bin/broker.exe

15. http://scienceblogs.com/deltoid/2001/07/27/levittpoolsvsguns/

16. CDC. WISQARS, see link for fn. 14.

17. https://www.afsp.org/understanding-suicide/facts-and-figures

18. Hemenway, "Risks and benefits," *op. cit.,* p. 504.

19. http://www.suicide.org/international-suicide-statistics.html

20. http://www.cdc.gov/mmwr/PDF/ss/ss5408.pdf

21. A. Kellerman, et. al., "Suicide in the home in relation to gun ownership," New England Journal of Medicine, (1992), 327, pp. 467-472; "Gun ownership as a risk factor for homicide in the Home," NEJM (1993), 329, pp. 1084-1091.

22. U. S. Department of Justice, Bureau of Investigation, Uniform Crime Reports for the United States and its Possessions,
Online: https://archive.org/details/uniformcrimerepo1932unit.

Chapter 5

1. Firearms and Violence, A Critical Review (Washington, 2005.)

2. The article on reasons for the 1990's decline in crime, along with Levitt's own theory about a connection between crime rates and Rove v. Wade can be found in Chapter 4 of Freakonomics. The book sold a gazillion copies so who am I to judge what he says?

3. Firearms and Violence, op. cit., pp. 16-17.

4.	ibid., p. 102

5.	ibid., p. 103

6.	Kleck & Gertz, op. cit., p. 161.

7.	Firearms, op. cit., p. 107

8.	ibid., p. 126.

9.	ibid., p. 150.

10.	ibid., p. 151

11.	Cf., Chapt. 3, fn. 14. Ayres & Donohue, "Shooting Down," op.cit.

12.	ibid., p. 1271

13.	ibid., p. 1281

14.	Lott, op. cit., p. 49.

15.	Marvin Wolfgang, eds., "Victim-Precipitated Criminal Homicides," The Sociology of Crime and Delinquency, 2nd edn. (New York: Wiley, 1970), p. 569.

16.	http://mediamatters.org/research/2013/03/12/the-nine-worst-claims-about-guns-from-john-lott/193014

17.	http://www.fbi.gov/news/stories/2014/september/fbi-releases-study-on-active-shooter-incidents/pdfs/a-study-of-active-shooter-incidents-in-the-u.s.-between-2000-and-2013

18.	Firearms Violence, op. cit., p. 20

19.	ibid. p. 49.

20.	Data on hi-cap magazines and crime suggests a connection insofar as the Police Executive Research Forum found that nearly 40% of all departments surveyed reported a noticeable increase in hi-capacity semi-auto handguns being used in crimes. Cf., Guns and Breaking New Ground Crime: (2010), p. 2.

21.	Cf., numerous publications from Wintemute's Violence Prevention Research Center at UC-Davis.

22.   The IOM report is available online: http://www.iom.edu/
Reports/2013/Priorities-for-Research-to-Reduce-the-Threat-of-
Firearm-Related-Violence.aspx

23.   Cf. Gallup: http://www.gallup.com/poll/165605/personal
-safety-top-reason-americans-own-guns-today.aspx

Chapter 6

1.   Home-grown hate groups like the posse have long been
the particular interest of the Southern Poverty Law
Center, cf., http://www.splcenter.org/get-informed/intelligence
-report/browse-all-issues/1998/spring/roots-of-common-law

2.   The Ruby Ridge 1992 incident in Northern Idaho was a
ten-day siege between Randy Weaver, a former Army engineer,
and agents from the FBI, ATF, Secret Service, local SWAT, state
police and other agencies. Weaver was subsequently defended by
the famed attorney Gerry Spence, and his account of the episode,
The Federal Siege of Ruby Ridge, along with numerous
documentaries, made him the poster-boy of the militia
movement.

3.   Cf., study by the SPLC: http://www.splcenter.org/get-
informed/publications/splc-report-return-of-the-militias.

4.   This quote was copied down from Nugent's Facebook
page on 9/3/14 but it was removed several days later.

5.   Cf., http://www.nytimes.com/interactive/2013/12/10/us
/state-gun-laws-enacted-in-the-year-since-newtown.html?_r=0

6.   http://www.atf.gov/sites/default/files/assets/Firearms/2
012-firearms-reported-lost-and-stolen.pdf.

7.   U.S. Department of Justice, "A Study of Active Shooter
Incidents in the United States Between 2000 and 2013."

ABOUT THE AUTHOR

Michael R. Weisser was born in Washington, D.C., educated in New York City public schools and received a Ph.D. in Economic History at Northwestern University. He is a featured blogger with Huffington Post and also blogs about guns at www.mikethegunguy.com. Since 1978 he has been a firearms retailer, wholesaler, law enforcement distributor and importer with total gun sales in excess of 30,000 handguns, rifles and shotguns. He is also a Life Member of the NRA and a certified firearms instructor in six specialties. He can be reached at his blog or at mike@mikethegunguy.com.

www.ingramcontent.com/pod-product-compliance
Lightning Source LLC
Chambersburg PA
CBHW030004290326
41934CB00005B/222